Paula Deen's
Savannah Style

with

Brandon Branch

Photographs by

Deborah Whitlaw Llewellyn

SIMON & SCHUSTER
New York London Toronto Sydney

SIMON & SCHUSTER
1230 Avenue of the Americas
New York, NY 10020

First Simon & Schuster hardcover edition April 2010

SIMON & SCHUSTER and colophon are registered trademarks of Simon & Schuster, Inc.

For information about special discounts for bulk purchases,
please contact Simon & Schuster Special Sales at
1-866-506-1949 or business@simonandschuster.com.

The Simon & Schuster Speakers Bureau can bring authors
to your live event. For more information or to book an event,
contact the Simon & Schuster Speakers Bureau at
1-866-248-3049 or visit our website at www.simonspeakers.com.

Designed by Pinafore Press / Janice Shay

Manufactured in the United States of America

1 3 5 7 9 10 8 6 4 2

Library of Congress Cataloging-in-Publication Data

Deen, Paula H.
Paula Deen's Savannah style / by Paula Deen with Brandon Branch;
with photographs by Deborah Whitlaw Llewellyn.
p. cm.
1. Interior decoration—Georgia—Savannah. I. Branch, Brandon.
II. Llewellyn, Deborah Whitlaw. III. Title.
IV. Title: Savannah style.
NK2011.S38 D44
747—dc22   2009038256

ISBN 978-1-4165-5224-6

This book is dedicated with love to Savannah, Georgia, my home. Savannah gave me a second chance at life, and the beauty, history, and hospitality of the city continue to inspire and sustain me.
—**Paula Deen**

This book is a living testament to all that my grandmother, Patsy Forbes, taught me about plants and flowers as a child. She passed on to me her passion for horticulture, as well as an appreciation for the finer things in life. Thank you, Mawmaw!
I thank my parents, Phillip and Sandra Branch, for making me milk the cows, which inspired me to go to college and get an education, and for instilling in me a hard-work ethic that serves me well.
Thanks also to my partner, Jim Johnston, for putting up with me at the end of many long days, and for taking good care of our four-legged children.
Jim, you are my strength and my soul mate.
My heartfelt thanks to Paula Deen for believing in me and allowing me to be a part of her family. Paula, I am eternally grateful for all that you've taught me.
—**Brandon Branch**

Acknowledgments

I was blessed to be able to work with a wonderful team of people on this book—quite a few cooks stirred the pot!

Thanks to Deborah Whitlaw Llewellyn and Janice Shay for their creative guidance and our shared love of Savannah; thanks also to Jamie Cribbs, my hairdressing genius; to Courtney Fix, my makeup goddess; to interior designer Carolyn Hultman, for her great taste and for sometimes knowing me as well as I know myself; to Christie Smith, for her lovely painted furniture; and special thanks and hugs to my wonderful assistant and coauthor, Brandon Branch.

To all the people who gave freely of their time and their beautiful homes, I want to thank Jane Coslick, Sarah Mieghen, Kelley and Greg Parker, Ellen Bolch, James Morton, Cathy Jarman, Paula Danyluk, Cynthia Hanks, Stephanie Lindley, Charlie Brown, Mary and Howard Morrison, Jeannie Sims, Mo Darden, Donna Foltz, and my own sweet boys, Jamie and Bobby Deen.

Thanks to our editor, Sydny Miner, a Yankee who appreciates Savannah style. And thanks to Michelle Rorke, Sybil Pincus, Nancy Singer, Jackie Seow, and everybody at Simon & Schuster, especially publisher David Rosenthal.

Table of Contents

Hi, y'all!

Savannah is a very special place to me and my family. For years I have brought the flavors of my kitchen to you; now it's time you got to know my hometown the way I do. I was born in Albany, Georgia, but Savannah became my "forever" home when I moved here in 1987. The wonderful old buildings and timeless Southern traditions just clicked with me, and I've never wanted to leave. When I went into the restaurant business in 1991, Savannah opened its arms and heart (as well as its pocketbooks!) and helped my restaurants and me become a success. Savannah is a place where traditional Southern cookin' fits right in. For that, I am truly grateful.

Savannah is where I raised my boys, found my true love, and welcomed my first grandbaby into this world, so I feel the city is a big part of my family life. I'm so happy to be able to show you my Savannah in this book—my own home, lots of my friends' beautifully decorated houses, and some of my favorite places and the things that are special to me, and I hope will be special for you. Don'tcha just love to peep into other people's houses and see how they live? I know I do! When I'm at home there's always a crowd of people there—friends, business associates who come to meet with me, television crews, either setting up or shutting down production for a show, and, of course, my menagerie of dogs and birds. Thank goodness my house is built to hold a load of people! It's not terribly big, but there are lots of tables, chairs, porches, outdoor seating areas, and nooks where we can gather and talk, eat or while away some time watchin' the water. I even have couches in my kitchen—why bother to leave my favorite room if I just need to rest a spell? And for that matter, why make my friends and family gather in another room while I'm fixin' dinner? I want them there with me, so my kitchen is obviously one of the most important rooms in my house and I'll be showing you why it's so special in the pages of this book.

Historic Savannah is a three-hundred-year-old city and the homes here have lots of things about them that make them different from houses in other Southern cities. It's a city that honors tradition and history and it's an old-fashioned walking city. When I lived downtown,

there were days I did not have to get into my car all day long; I could walk to work at the Lady & Sons! I moved to Wilmington Island in 2001 to be closer to the water. The marshes, water, rivers, creeks, and salt-sea air around here are invigorating, and my new condo felt like a retreat from all the work at the restaurant. The new development had been designed to look like the town houses in the downtown historic district, so I felt I had the best of both worlds.

Savannah and I are a lot alike. I know it sounds odd, but we do have lots of things in common. Consider this: Savannah embraces quirky characters (thank the Lord!), likes things with a little bit of age to them, and loves its Southern traditions. Sound familiar? Honey, I was home the moment I arrived.

I hope you enjoy the special homes I show you in this book. I love them and I think you will, too. My wonderful, amazing assistant and designer, Brandon Branch, will tell you how you can use these Savannah lifestyle ideas for your own home, so you can bring a little Savannah into your life, too.

Lots of love from my home to yours, y'all!

Paula Deen

It makes me so happy to bring

Savannah style to you with this book. In each of the chapters, I will be sharing ideas with you on how to bring a little bit of our Low Country look into your home, no matter where you live. Savannah style is a mix of antique and new, casual and formal, and lives lived as much and as often outside the home as inside.

The secret to a great-looking, comfortable space is to focus on the little things: bunches of seasonal flowers, fun flea market and yard sale treasures, chandeliers in every room you can imagine, plants in all the right places, and fabulous, eclectic pieces of furniture that tell a story about you.

You'll see how flowers and plants influence the look of a room; how to add color to create a mood; how to make a personal collection the focal point of a room, and much, much more.

I am blessed to be able to work closely with Paula, and over the years I have touched every part of her public life—helping choose her wardrobe, arranging her flowers, and choosing table settings to be filmed and photographed for her shows and magazines.

And, finally, I hope you like Paula's own furniture designs that are found in some of these rooms. Paula and I worked closely with manufacturers to make sure that each piece has her down-home touch, and her wonderful sense of Savannah style.

Spring

Don'tcha just love it when you first know that spring is here? I know y'all have your own sweet memories of the season, but it just seems to me that everyone loves spring because it is such a happy time. Or maybe it's such a happy time because everyone loves spring—I don't know which! I know *I'm* happy for lots of reasons that time of year. It's hard to be sad when the weather finally gives us a break and warms up enough so we can head outdoors again. Of course, we're spoiled here in Savannah because we have such warm weather, but usually by March we've gotten tired of the few cold spells we suffer; the wool clothes are beginning to feel kinda dreary, and we're ready for the sun and the time to be in it.

My house suddenly becomes much bigger in the warm weather, when we can use my front and back porches. They're two of the best rooms of the house when the weather's right. Then there's what I call my "back-yard resort," which is my new dock house. I'll tell you more about that special place later—it is close to my heart and it's only one room!

At the first sign of warm weather, I pull one of my rocking chairs out onto the porch, prop up a comfy pillow, and relocate my birds to their front porch aviary because I know they're as tired of being cooped up as I am. They let me know how happy they are by singing and cuttin' up a fuss. And, of course, my five dog-babies are always right there with me, too, sniffing the flowers and peein' on the pansies!

Spring means lots of things going on inside and outside Savannah homes that make them special. Flowers are front and center, all over town in gardens, window boxes, porches, and hidden gardens, and seen in luscious little glimpses behind wrought-iron gates in our historic downtown.

Outdoor furniture is pulled out of the garage, uncovered, and spruced up to be ready for company on St. Patrick's Day (spring does come early here), Easter, Mother's Day, and all the family birthdays and occasions we celebrate. We go all out on porch decor, and some of my friends even hang chandeliers out on the porch, which makes cocktail hour outdoors at dusk seem wicked elegant. There's lots to show you about spring livin' in Savannah, so here goes!

I just about live on my front and back porches during the springtime, and I like to make sure that the furniture is comfortable—and durable, too. That means lots of wicker that can be easily cleaned, lots of plants, and a few ceiling fans to keep it cool.

Rockin' on the Water

This is my new favorite place to be. And before you say that rocking chairs are a symbol of old age, let me just set you straight: everybody likes to rock, young and old. The act of falling asleep in someone's arms in a rocking chair must be buried deep in our Southern psyche. I'm sure it's the reason that kids like rocking chairs as much as adults. I know that whenever I'd be sittin' in a rocker, my kids—and now my beautiful grandbaby, Jack—couldn't wait to crawl right up in my lap and snuggle me. That's a sweet memory of those boys.

Life is grand, isn't it? No matter where I am, when the day is over and I want to put up my feet and relax, the place I long for most is my porch, with Michael, my dogs, and something delicious to nibble on while I watch the sunset over the creek. Lord, don't we love the simple things? These days, it seems like we're all too busy to take a moment of quiet time and enjoy a good rocker. I'm blessed to have work that I love, but I still cherish my private weekends when I can sneak out onto the porch and just sit and let the water and sun relax me. Forget spas—this is how to live the good life!

You can find all sorts of things on Savannah porches, and my favorites always seem to be a flea market find or a garage sale treasure—in this case, a candelabra to help create a romantic mood for a porch supper. I love my big bunch of blooms in the window box, too. Just goes to show that you can enjoy spring flowers anywhere.

Porch Livin'

Porches come in all shapes and sizes around Savannah, and I think they are great spots for family fun. Regardless of how grand or humble a house in the South may be, you can bet we always have a porch of some sort. Southerners love the outdoors; with semitropical weather, Savannahians enjoy all sorts of outdoor entertainment year-round.

In the spring and summer, a porch can be a party room, game room, dining room, parlor, or just the best place to grab a catnap. It's where the kids and the pets feel free to play as they please without the adults worrying and fretting over whether anything will be broken or stained. And you can't beat the cost: a porch is cooled by natural breezes and lit by the warm sun. The hum of sturdy ceiling fans lulls you, and the sweet smells of spring can be enjoyed without the help of a plug-in scent. You just can't beat those environmental pluses!

In the spring, I pull a couple of blankets out onto the porch to air out and soon find that a porch swing, a book, and a blanket are my new best friends.

If the porch is on the front or side of the house, as many are in downtown

The table is set with my own dinnerware, inspired by the marsh grasses you can see from this very porch. The big glass flutes on the outdoor chandelier hold water and fragrant lemons.

Porch furniture is slipcovered with a durable outdoor fabric so that it lasts and lasts. New pillows update the look seasonally. The gas lanterns flanking the double front doors are reproductions of an old New Orleans gaslight.

Historic Savannah, the room becomes a meeting and greeting place for neighbors and friends, both old and new, and anyone strolling by who starts a conversation and has the time to visit.

I believe the offer to "come in and sit a spell" must have originally been coined for the friend who was in need of a porch, a rocker, and a cool drink—in just that order!

Brandon's Style Secrets

Porches are for bringing your lifestyle outside during the warm months. You should think of the porch as an extra room, and like any other room in your house, it should reflect your sense of style. Be creative—think of your porch as a nighttime room as well as a daytime space. Use candles and lanterns to add drama and romance to the porch, or consider moving a comfortable couch and chairs outside if you're entertaining in the evening.

Use lots of pillows and fabrics on outdoor couches and chairs to update old pieces. This will allow you to change your look seasonally for very little money.

Tired of that old furniture but don't want to have it restored? Dress it up with a slipcover that you can pull off and launder whenever you need to freshen it up.

Lighting is important for an inviting porch. Pull some lamps out and use them on your porch when you have guests over. Don't be afraid to go over the top with these "borrowed" pieces—the fancier the better, for that air of Southern decadence!

Outdoor rugs are no longer plain, dreary remainders. Rugs define an outdoor space, so look at new colorful patterns to dress up your porch furniture. I like Paula's collection because of the range of outdoor botanical patterns, color, and traditional patterns.

Step through the shuttered door panels into the Parkers' classy Southern side porch. Cane chairs and a comfortable settee; a marble-topped, iron-trimmed table, exterior gaslights, and classical column details combine to make this side porch the perfect place to unwind over drinks and a late brunch. The porch overlooks the courtyard side garden, complete with a tinkling fountain.

The shuttered wall ensures privacy but allows breezes in to cool the porch. The oversize gas lantern, opposite, is a beautiful, old-fashioned way to light a porch in the evening— the closest thing to candlelight. It's so very romantic!

With a large seating area on one side and plush teak daybeds on the other, the Lindleys' large front porch doubles as a sitting room and a place for a languid afternoon nap. The outdoor curtains can be pulled closed for greater privacy. This porch is dressed up and ready for a cocktail party, with candles and cut flowers. Painted or stained teak can be used outdoors without ruining the wood.

Stephanie and Jim Lindley's porch at their Isle of Hope cottage looks directly out onto the Wilmington River and is their preferred place to entertain. Area rugs, plush furniture, elegant silver lamps, and chandeliers dress up the space.

Screened Porches

Ever heard of no-see-'ums? You might want to know this about the South: if you're gonna sit outside in the spring and summer—and sometimes the fall—you need to put a little bit of screen between you, the skeeters, and the no-see-'ums. The upside to having your porch screened is that you can treat it like an extension of your house. Need another guest room? A dining room? With screens on your porch, you can enjoy the room without the elements intruding too much. A little rain is nice to enjoy while sitting on a screened-in porch.

Jane Coslick moved to Tybee beach in 1992 and started designing and restoring the typical small cottages dotting the island. To date, she's redone thirty-eight cottages, and has purchased eight for herself. Her designs have become synonymous with Tybee's casual beach style.

In the cottage at right, Jane used Sunbrella fabric for the curtains, which won't mildew or fade. Her favorite things in the room are the big daybed pillows, which she made out of chenille palm tree shower curtains. She recycles old furniture and paints the pieces her signature bright beachy color, which will cheer you up just looking at them.

Screened porches are like tree houses: they bring out the kid in us and make us do silly things, like put hula skirts on the daybed. This wonderful room doubles as a guest bedroom in spring and summer.

Porch Views

Screened or unscreened, covered or uncovered, on the front, side, or back of the house, porches all have one thing in common: they are good for seeing and being seen. Naturally, you would expect Savannahians to come up with a bushel of ways to do this, and we have. Walk down any street in downtown Savannah and you'll see parlor-level porches; gaze through the fence and you will see the side porches; get yourself invited in and you'll see the courtyard and balcony porches. Southerners do enjoy the outdoors, which usually means sitting comfortably with a drink and a smile. Having a good view from the porch is a real plus!

The porch at the far left is seen from the landing of a town house's parlor floor. These little front porches on historic downtown town houses are only big enough to hold a love seat or chair but are great for viewing the street action, waving to the tour buses, and greeting the dog walkers.

Below, Jeannie Sims's lovely sitting room opens onto a balcony porch with a view of her tiny, jewel-like enclosed garden.

Right, the Brennans' classic side porch is the neighborhood's favorite spot from which to have a drink and watch the St. Patrick's Day parade as it winds around the city's squares.

Courtyard Gardens & More

It seems like everyone in Savannah must have a garden; this is a city of flowers and well-planned gardens, both large and small. It's no coincidence that I've used Brandon's beautiful seasonal flower arrangements for each of the four seasons in this book. You won't go into a home in Savannah that doesn't proudly show off the blossoms from its garden.

When the camellias start to bloom in late January, it seems to everyone that we've beaten winter. Spring here lasts from late February until the end of May, and Savannahians take advantage of the weather to work and play outside most of the year. Gardening can be both to those of us who love it.

Everyone holds their breath hopin' that the azaleas will be out by St. Patrick's Day when all the visitors arrive. We just love to show off our gardens!

I used to come home after a long day at the restaurant and unwind in the little courtyard of my sweet historic town house. I just loved that town house! It was barely big enough for me and my birds and it suited me fine. When I opened The Lady & Sons in downtown Savannah, I was working day and night

The size of a courtyard garden in Savannah is never important; rather, it's how well dressed it is that counts. This little spot is bedecked with jeweled chandeliers for light in the evening, and a mirrored back gate to reflect all the exotic palms, ferns, and orchids in the tiny space. Just right for a cool glass of sweet tea, y'all!

The Parkers' side garden is a great example of "designing up" to visually enlarge the space. A nook in the tall garden wall holds an urn, and the eighteen-foot-high wrought-iron columns draw the eye upward.

Brandon's Style Secrets

Don't be afraid of converting a small outdoor space to a garden, even if you don't have a green thumb or a lot of dirt. The size of the space need not define what you do.

Nowhere is it written that gardens need to be filled with seasonal flowers. In small spaces you can decorate the walls and create a visual depth with creeping fig vine. Of course, pots of flowers are always colorful if you like them, so feel free to decorate with color.

Add a mirror to a gate or wall, or behind a fountain, to give the illusion of more space in the garden.

Don't be afraid to use old lawn furniture that is rusty or has chipped paint. Courtyard furniture shouldn't be mint perfect. A worn look is very good!

Do you have a large garden area but would like the feel of a small courtyard garden instead? Use architectural elements to define a small space within your garden, and treat it as a separate garden "room." Arbors, trellises, walls, and columns are all ways that you can visually create a small, intimate garden.

When you've created your perfect private garden, don't be afraid to use it. Invite some friends over for drinks and enjoy!

I love all the carved and cast animals you can see around Savannah decorating walls, gardens, and porches. This old lion, peeking out from under the ivy wall at the Parkers' home, doesn't scare me. He gets a lot of petting from passersby, I'll bet. Savannah has a wealth of little details like Mr. Lion that are fun to discover.

to make ends meet and I needed a calm place to go to when I had a little time to myself. It's probably a good thing that I didn't have a great big ol' bedroom at that time of my life because when I hit my bed, I was sound asleep. Instead, my courtyard became my favorite place to unwind and relax after a hard day.

Nothin' beats being surrounded by flowers and green things. I love working in the garden I have now on Wilmington Island. It's no tiny courtyard garden—it's a pretty good size (you may have seen it if you've watched *Cooking with Paula Deen*), and I have a kitchen garden, too.

The main garden is in the English style, but it's not as big as a traditional English garden. I don't have the time these days to maintain a huge garden, but I love the flowers, vegetables, and fruit I grow. My kitchen garden is tucked right into the flower garden and is surrounded by boxwoods to mark the perimeters. I grow herbs, tomatoes, broccoli, and cabbage in season, and there are big containers near my back door that hold collards and leeks. I have pear trees in containers that I'll take with me to the new house when I move.

But let's get back to downtown so I can tell you about courtyard gardens and the hidden gardens that are so typical of Savannah style. The space between the town house and the carriage house

James Morton's walled 60- by 100-foot green garden on East Jones Street was started in 1974. Seen from the street through a nineteenth-century wrought-iron gate, it was one of the largest gardens in the historic district.

on a typical lot in Historic Savannah was used as a workspace hundreds of years ago. The spaces are all small, usually no larger than thirty by thirty feet. The land was historically used for day-to-day needs such as cooking and washing. With the advent of the twentieth century, modern amenities allowed this work to move inside the house, and the space evolved into gardens. Most of those courtyard gardens are surrounded by tall walls of gray brick, and this privacy allowed these gardens to become private refuges and,

The greenhouse at Lebanon Plantation is not only a great place for cultivating Mary Morrison's orchids and flowering plants, it's a sweet spot for afternoon tea, too. The last time we were there, around the Christmas holidays, the greenhouse was decorated with its own little tree to light it up.

My spring garden, at right, is defined with little gravel paths. I love to walk through the hip-deep blossoms this time of year and cut whatever I need for the house. I don't have as much time to garden as I'd like, but it is one of my favorite pastimes, not what I call work at all.

in essence, another room in which to entertain, which is a pastime only exceeded in popularity by gardening in Savannah.

The garden walls kept passersby from seeing into the gardens, but there are many who want to share the beauty of their handiwork with others. These people have installed wrought-iron gates or wooden doors with little windows that afford the curious a peek into the garden. Keep your eyes open on a slow stroll down any Savannah street and you will find many of these hidden treasures.

Other courtyard gardens can be seen only from the lanes. (Savannah alleys are called "lanes," in the English tradition, rather than "alleys.") The lanes are all named; many of the old carriage houses open onto a lane rather than a major street, so it's easier for the mailman to find these houses if they have their own address. Each spring, there is a hidden-garden tour, held by the garden club called N.O.G.S., which stands for "north of Gaston Street," the area that is the downtown historic district. It is so much fun to get that map of all the hidden gardens on the tour and then steal down the lanes to find all the beautiful gardens that most people never see. It's one of my favorite Savannah festivals.

A view of James Morton's garden gazebo, above, shows one of the many lovely spots packed into this walled garden. The 60- by 100-foot lot is small by some standards, but large for our historic downtown.

This is Jeannie Sims's little courtyard—the same garden I was drinking tea in at the beginning of this chapter. It shows the double doors that open from her kitchen onto the space. The 15- by 18-foot space is packed with exotic plants, two koi ponds, orchids, and a perfect table for visiting and relaxing.

Wonderful garden decorations are, clockwise from upper left: the dogs' water fountain in my own garden (you can see it accommodates both large and small dogs); a sweet sentimental stone message planted in the Morrisons' garden near their greenhouse; fun little birdhouses attached to a palm tree on the beach at Tybee Island; and two sweet statues almost hidden by vines and ferns in downtown courtyards.

Brandon's Style Secrets

Gardens need focal points other than just growing things, and almost anything goes in Savannah gardens as long as it's pretty or fun. The key to using small garden statuary, bird houses, and even fountains or water features is to almost hide them. Tucked away in a corner of the garden or along a path, they should be a surprise that delights and intrigues.

Garden ornaments don't have to cost a lot of money. Don't be afraid to buy statues and sculptures that you like, even if they look as if they just came off the showroom floor. You can create a patina of age on a new piece of statuary by coating it with this formula: blend equal parts potting soil and yogurt to make a sludge and rub it onto the new statue. (Wear rubber gloves!) Concentrate on filling the nooks and crannies well to give it depth and age. If you add a bit of sheet moss into the mixture, the seeds will germinate in the sludge and grow moss on your statue. You'll have an instant antique that will look as if it's been in your garden for decades.

Keep an eye out at yard sales and antique stores and auctions for unusual pieces that will become a conversation starter in your garden. Anything goes, as long as you like it, and these personalize your garden.

Wrought Iron

You probably think of New Orleans when you think of wrought iron, but you'd be surprised at how much of it can be seen right here in Savannah. Wrought-iron and cast-iron staircases, banisters, newel posts, window frames and ornamentation, gates, doors, chandeliers, downspouts, drain covers, garden furniture, and ornaments can all be seen just walking down Jones Street at the center of the historic district. Some of the designs are as old as the hills, just like the homes, and some are new designs made by contemporary artisans who keep the craft alive.

I love the garden gates the most

The banister at left is a modern alternative to the traditional wrought iron seen on some of the older homes in Savannah. Ivan Bailey is locally famous for his wrought-iron workmanship. Although Bailey no longer lives here, he ran a forge in Savannah from 1972 to 1983 and created many of the beautiful wrought-iron gates, banisters, and garden sculptures we enjoy today.

Opposite, ornamental vines, heavy with fruit, grace the gate to a downtown garden and is a hint of what is grown inside.

because they are such a tease when you're sightseeing downtown. No matter how long you've lived here, it's impossible to walk down a street and not sneak a look behind that garden gate or into that big open window just to see what it looks like inside! You won't be disappointed; we Savannahians like to show off our pretty things. Nothing is left to chance—the gate is designed to catch your eye first, so that you look farther into the garden to appreciate the flowers, the fountain, or a hundred different details that can be glimpsed as you stroll from house to house.

It always tickles me to see the little round decorative window insets at the street level, because they must have been dreamed up by a cook. You see, during the nineteenth century the kitchens were on the ground level, and when the cook put her pies near the window to cool, eager little hands could easily make off with the goodies. Some clever woman must have discovered that a wrought-iron inset in the window would keep thieving hands out of the pie and still allow the breezes to cool her kitchen! Of course, I'll bet you anything there were some softhearted cooks like me who would put a plate of little treats near that window so the kids could think they were getting away with something anyway! Wouldn't you?

The first time I lived in a house downtown, I had to get over the feeling that

The lovely home below is a double house, so the original architect included matching wrought-iron porch "walls." The wrought iron is structural as well as decorative, and the overall feel is lacy and airy. The view of the square it looks into is not impeded by anything but the delicate designs of the wrought iron.

The creatively pierced metal chandelier opposite was designed for Lebanon Plantation by the owner's grandmother, herself an artist. It hangs in the big gathering room of the guesthouse, and whimsically depicts fishermen in the Low Country. Lamps on the ends of tiny chains hang from the fishing rods.

A simple iron gate allows a full view of the garden it encloses, which is a treat for tourists and neighbors alike. Sculptural birds cavort for our entertainment just beyond the gate.

With a gate as beautiful as this one, it doesn't even matter what the garden holds. You can get lost in appreciation of the detail and craftsmanship.

Brandon's Style Secrets

You can find wrought iron and decorative metal pieces from a variety of sources: stores, catalogs, auctions, antique stores, and, of course, flea markets and yard sales. Don't be afraid to use an inexpensive substitute for wrought iron if cost is an issue. The look is very similar, and most pieces can be painted, just like wrought iron, to create your own look. Most Savannah wrought iron is painted black or Charleston green, which is a very, very dark green/black, but you can use your own imagination.

Consider wrought-iron gates and decorative details to be outdoor artwork, and feature them as such. These are not the pieces that you want to hide in the back of the garden!

If you live in a city and don't have a garden, using wrought-iron pieces indoors can lend a Southern garden feel. Try using a wrought-iron gate for a headboard to your bed, or use a fence detail for a wall hanging. Perhaps a balcony door could be made of glass and wrought iron, rather than wood.

Wrought-iron details such as this circular flower design are cleverly used to focus our gaze— in this case, on the sculpture and circular fountain just inside.

the decorative wrought iron on the windows was just a security measure. In Albany, if you put iron bars on a window, it meant you were afraid somebody was gonna try to get in. I realized that the wrought iron in Savannah windows had other uses when I saw that, unless there was ironwork detail to keep them in, the dogs could jump out the big windows that went almost to the floor. So, that turned my idea around—the ironwork wasn't there to keep people out, it was to keep the kids and dogs in.

Traditional stairways, banisters, and balcony details join the list of other wrought-iron features in Historic Savannah: downspouts, gates, newel posts, window insets, garden furniture, and more.

Wicker

As Southern as peach pie, and just as easy to find on any porch, parlor, or dining room around town, wicker furniture is a staple in Savannah homes. Wicker is a no-brainer for anyone who lives on the coast, because it's casual, durable, and relatively cheap. Michael always says you can treat it like you would your wife on a Saturday night! Our wicker furniture sits out on the porch the whole winter long, and then after a quick cleanup, it's ready for spring before you can say "Lord love a duck, but it's hot out!"

I dress up my wicker chairs and sofas with patterned pillows and slipcovers, and change the look often enough to fool myself into thinking I have new furniture.

The dogs can't be fooled, of course. They get to sit on the wicker furniture because it's easy to clean, so they know their favorite chair whether it's fluffed up with new pillows or not. I scatter little dog beds throughout the house for their comfort (I'm a fool for these dogs!), but you can bet they're up on the wicker chairs just as often as they're in their beds.

Both my front and back porches are

I love all the green, green, green on my porch. It is a perfectly fresh spring look to complement the white wicker furniture I have scattered around both my porches. I change the slipcovers if I want a new look, and I always scatter colorful pillows around to brighten things up.

The porch swing opposite is hung from chains and, I can tell you from experience, is a great place for an afternoon nap. The dogs have their own little bed close by, and the casual look is all pulled together with one of my outdoor rugs with a fern and flower pattern, called Beaufort Linen. I love these outdoor rugs because they are so pretty and yet they can be scrubbed and scoured

without hurting them at all. Great for dogs and kids!

With all the great wicker furniture, the enclosed porch at Lebanon Plantation still has the feel of an outdoor porch. The darker green color gives a more formal look to the room, which is decorated with wonderful art, books, antique chandeliers, and family treasures.

long and wide, so I've got lots of wicker furniture sitting out, ready for visitors and family to fall onto and stretch out on. And I want y'all to notice my new outdoor carpets. They are a real pretty way to make the porch feel like a proper room. Just like the wicker pieces, you can wash these carpets when they get dirty. I take a hose to them, and really scrub them clean and they keep on looking great.

There's always a formal side to Savannah living, and wicker can be used in a more elegant setting, too. The Morrisons' Lebanon Plantation has big, wide wraparound porches that they've enclosed

with lots of windows. The overall look is so bright and light that it still feels like an outdoor porch, and the wicker furniture carries that thought through. They've also added wonderful artwork, sculpture, fine lamps, and other nice things that couldn't take the weather on an open porch.

The one-thousand-acre Lebanon Plantation boasts a big main house and a few small old cabins that have various uses. The Morrisons say that their grandkids' favorite cabin for playing is the old washhouse, which is furnished with all sorts of mismatched garden furniture and wicker pieces.

All the cushions, rugs, paintings, and ceramic pieces that are in the cabin are decorated with flower motifs, so the cabin is nicknamed The Flower Cottage. With no screens on the old windows, you can be sure that there'll be a few bees buzzing around the "flowers" inside when you're relaxing there on a summer day!

As I mentioned at the start of this chapter, my little dock house is my favorite hidey-hole for a weekend getaway, or whenever I can sneak away.

I have to tell you a little bit about this cabin. It was on the dock when we purchased the land, but it was in sad shape. It had low ceilings, too-small rooms, and was in real disrepair. I decided to make it livable again, so we opened up the eight-foot ceilings to a height of fifteen feet; Robert Meadows, who was helping with the restoration, found wood from his grandmother's 125-year-old farmhouse to mix with the original wood walls that could be salvaged. Our trim carpenter, James Aikens, used the farmhouse wood for the new walls, and put the salvaged wood from the original dock house on the raised walls. Robert also put a zinc roof on the building and made a wonderful table for us with a bottom made out of an old wooden crab trap and a zinc top.

The footprint of the cabin had to remain historically correct to comply with building codes for these old structures. We took out all the walls and made it essentially a one-room cabin, and Michael and I love the result.

We realized, sadly, that we'd forgotten to take pictures of the "before" cabin. When it had just been completed, Michael went to the marina nearby to pick up something, and he just happened upon a book there that had a photo of the cabin in its state of disrepair. We were so excited to find this

This tiny cabin is just jam-packed with things that mean a bunch to me. I had my momma's couch reupholstered special for this place. I've kept it for, I don't know, more than forty years. I love it so much! I don't like to part with things that mean a lot to me, and I always think of Momma when I see my pretty couch.

TYBEE 18

These two bamboo wicker chairs were a flea market find, and I love them so much, they became the first things I put in my little dock house. No need to do refinishing or anything to fancy them up. They give it a retro look, which suits me just fine.

beautiful book with a "before" picture of our new "old" dock house, and it sits on Robert's zinc table now for everyone to see.

Since the cabin's right on the water, I knew I wanted some wicker chairs to make it look like a casual retreat. I love my old red bamboo chairs that I've had for ages, so I brought them to the cabin. It gave just the right feel to this old-fashioned little hideaway, and, in fact, everything else is designed around these two old red chairs.

Although you see a lot of new wicker these days, wicker has an old-fashioned appeal to it. That's because it's been around for more than a century.

Wicker was really popular in the nineteenth century, during Victorian times. Wicker furniture was designed originally for both indoor and outdoor use. The simplicity of the material meant that it could be woven into many different shapes, styles, and designs. The Victorians even had wicker baby carriages, which I still see occasionally in antique stores and at auctions.

The reason for the success of wicker, though, is the simple fact that it can be enjoyed outdoors. You just don't worry about wicker staying out in the rain, and Savannahians, like everyone, enjoy things that don't take much effort and worry.

It's also easy to paint, so if you have an old piece that you'd like to spruce

Outdoor curtains are inexpensive and create a romantic sense of privacy, not to mention shelter from the hot part of the day. A wicker chair, the rustle of palm fronds, the gentle movement of a curtain blowing in the breeze—it's all I need to relax.

up, it's an easy job with a can of spray paint. White always seems to be popular at the beach, and it's a rare porch or sunroom that doesn't have a piece of wicker furniture. You can update an old piece by just throwing on a slip-cover, which is what I do. It covers up a multitude of condition problems, and looks great.

This little cabin away from the main house at Lebanon Plantation is mainly for the Morrisons' grandkids and family to rest and play. It is nicknamed The Flower Cottage, and everything with flowers and wicker seems to have ended up here, as well as the metal garden furniture. Having served for so long outdoors, it is enjoying indoor retirement now. The casual mix of wicker and garden furniture is inviting to the grandkids when they visit. And having their own little cabin to play and read in is irresistible.

Not only will you find wonderful, worn old wicker pieces in this little cabin at Lebanon Plantation, but the porcelain birdcage on the table mimics a wicker design. It is all so Southern!

Summer

If you like it hot, and anyone who

cooks learns to enjoy the heat in the kitchen, then this city is for you. Even though I celebrate all four seasons, it never gets real cold here. That's a nice thing for those of us who can't take snow, but the flip side of this latitude is that summers are somethin' else! It is hotter than a June bride here during the summer, and the only way to escape the heat is to head to the water. Luckily, the Low Country boasts a bushel of creeks and rivers, and we have Tybee beach when we need to cool off with a little dip.

In 2006 I moved from my little house in downtown Savannah to a house on Turner's Creek at Wilmington Island. In just a ten-minute drive from the city to the water, the temperature can drop five whole degrees! That's just one of the reasons I am so happy livin' on the water that I never want to leave. At the time I'm writing this, I'm building a new house nearby, right on the Wilmington River. I needed a larger place to accommodate our film crews and equipment, much of which has to be hung from the ceiling. My old house just wasn't designed for that sort of thing.

I realized I really wanted a getaway place, too, which is why I renovated my little dock house. When I walk out there, sit on the dock, and talk to the dolphins, I just leave all my troubles behind. A getaway place is a great stress reliever, and I am blessed to have this cabin that reminds me so much of my childhood.

My granddaddy used to love his sleeping porch as a getaway place. He looked forward to the warm nights that allowed him to sleep outside (or the hot, hot nights he didn't have to sleep inside!), and, of course, us kids thought that spending a night on the sleeping porch was great fun—almost as good as camping. Lately, I'm pleased to see more and more sleeping porches turning up on new houses as well as some of the older ones being used again.

Not everyone likes the Savannah heat, but summer at our house is one big fun outdoor party on the water. In fact, my boys agree that the only thing better than a hot summer day is a cold glass of homemade lemonade!

Downtown Savannah is a great walking neighborhood, so there are always lots of customers for a fledgling lemonade business.

Dock vs. Deck

My favorite summer party is a dock party or a deck party. This is the best that the Low Country has to offer. All you need is a few friends, a place near the water, some comfortable seating, an umbrella or a roof over your head, and a mess of shrimp and crabs to boil. My mouth is already waterin'! You see docks all over the city, because Savannah is in the middle of a whole bunch of creeks, streams, and marshes that empty into the ocean. Where

The Lindleys' dock house, on the Isle of Hope, is a simple covered area with fans and comfortable outdoor furniture, as well as lounges for sunning on the water. With tables and various seating areas, it is perfect for parties.

The Parkers' Tybee Island deck butts right up to beach dunes for easy access to the water. The stone fireplace is the centerpiece of the deck and allows the family to enjoy outdoor dining in all seasons.

there's a boat, there's a dock. And where there's a dock, there's usually a dock house. The prettiest docks, to me, are on the Isle of Hope, and the dock houses there are always busy on a summer's evening.

Stephanie and Jim Lindley entertain outdoors constantly in the summer months at their Isle of Hope home, and they have a great view of the sunset from their dock house. It's fitted with ceiling fans, a bar with running water, a refrigerator, and lots of comfortable chairs for their guests.

Don't underestimate the value of a deck if you don't live near the water. We have a covered deck in back of our house on Turner's Creek, and it has become our summertime kitchen. It is equipped with everything my main kitchen has and is our

Below, the Brennans renovated a little-used part of their walled garden to include a brick patio and outdoor fireplace. The arbor, painted to match the Charleston green Adirondack chairs, defines the space.

favorite place to cook up barbecue and Low Country boils.

I will give you a little piece of advice, from my recent experience. Before you build, take a look at the many new products to use for decking. We used a product called Trex for our dock house decking. It's made from recycled garbage bags mixed with a wood by-product. It's strong, impervious to mold and rot, and insects won't bother it—plus, it's perfectly "green." But the best part for me is there are no splinters, so I can go barefoot when I feel like it.

Eat-in Kitchens

I've always loved eat-in kitchens.

I just seem to live around my stove, I guess. If I'm cookin', I want to be able to gab and laugh with my friends and family, and having a table in another room is just too far away from me. Or maybe I just don't like to waste any time getting the food from the stove to the table. Whatever the case, it just seems so natural to eat in the same place that you cook the food.

When the kids were young, there was never a question of whether we should eat in the dinin' room or the kitchen; we just had a table in the kitchen and that was that. Lots of folks eat that way, and grew up eatin' that way, and it just feels right. It doesn't matter if the table is a little bitty thing that fits into a corner of the room, or if it's a built-in banquette-style table like the one the Parkers have in their house in the historic district. I like to eat where I'm comfortable and I'll bet you do, too.

These habits are ingrained in me because of the way I was brought up. Although not wealthy by any means, my immediate family in Albany lived comfortably. My father was from more humble beginnings. His parents worked

This kitchen was redesigned to include the long trestle table, which seats ten people. The space is formal, with its monogrammed, slipcovered dining chairs; however, the abundant natural light attracts people and cats at all times.

A tiny breakfast nook can become the family's favorite place for everything, including visiting with the chef while dinner's cooking. The curved, banquette-style wooden base is made comfortable with cushions and pillows.

in an orange factory, peeling fruit, and they led a simple life; they were the salt of the earth. Many Southerners lived this way. It was a fact of life that a family would eat together in the kitchen, and that image still holds a simple sweetness for me to this day.

In my little dock house, the kitchen table is pushed up right beside the old farmhouse sink, in full view of the open shelves of plates, jams, jellies, coffee, cereal, and whatnot. I like a room that is not only comfortable to eat in but holds a few things that are dear to me, something special to me that makes me smile when I look at it. The thing that does that for me in the dock house cabin is a little Popeye lamp that sits right next to the stove. When I was visiting Katie Lee and Billy Joel, I saw the lamp in Billy's office and just made a big fuss over it, it was so cute. You see, Popeye reminds me of Michael. So Billy Joel said I had to have it and it has found a home next to where I cook. There are lots of pluses to having an informal eat-in kitchen, and lots of ways that you can make it special. In the summer, it can be the sunniest place in the house if you put your table near good windows. The Parkers' family cat uses their long trellis table as a sunroom when the table isn't in use otherwise.

Brandon's Style Secrets

Whether you have a large kitchen or a small one, tucking a table into a corner of the room with banquette-style seating, or designing a large space to include a generous table close to the cooking action, is a great way to enjoy a kitchen.

If your seating is built into the wall, use lots of pillows and durable cushions to make the area look inviting and comfortable. Use an upholstery fabric on your cushions that can be thrown into the washer. If you have a traditional dining table in your kitchen, make sure you have casual slipcovers, so the look is not too formal.

Of course, if you have a formal table in your kitchen, just make sure the rest of the kitchen is an extension of the style. Dress up your kitchen as you would any room.

Remember, the best thing to have in a kitchen is lots of light. If the room is not situated for good natural light, then choose lamps, chandeliers, and other light fixtures to brighten the area. Dimmer switches will allow you to have a romantic dinner in your eat-in kitchen, which is especially great if your home is short on space.

I put all my favorite cast-iron pots and skillets in the cabin, and keep them out to show. Having and displaying pieces with a story is important to me; it keeps me grounded and happy. The Popeye lamp on the countertop was a gift from Billy Joel and Katie Lee, and makes me smile when I remember both their generosity and their sense of humor.

Of course, an eat-in kitchen doesn't need to be an old-fashioned trip down memory lane, either. Lots of Savannah homes with a view out onto the water in back are designed as big, open spaces with built-in banquette dining. Whether the tables are big or small, they can be as elegant or as simple as your family likes. With this arrangement, you get the familial congeniality of cooking and eating in the same room, and you have the added plus of a beautiful view.

Space is at a premium in my little cabin kitchen, but there's a lot to look at on the walls and open shelves. The busy look works well in this tiny space, because the high ceiling allowed me to put more things on the walls.

Slipcovers

If you think everyone in Savannah spends their time polishing the silver and cleaning the antique fabric on Grandmomma's dining chairs, then you're wrong. We Southern women may be greatly attached to our family heirlooms, and we may love showing them off any chance we get, but given the choice of a day spent cleaning or a day out shopping and havin' fun, you just gotta know which one we'll always choose.

Furniture doesn't clean itself, but a slipcover can hide just about any accident. Sometimes I just don't want to explain about that stain where the dog threw up last week. It doesn't bother me, but it might ruin your appetite, so I prefer to hide it. The best thing to do when you're tired of your old furniture, or just want to protect it from kids, animals, and other guests, is to pull out the slipcovers and throw them on.

When the weather gets hot here and everyone at our house hits the water, I know its time to bring out the slipcovers. This practice is a summer tradition on the islands around Savannah. Wet suits, sand, dogs, barbecue sauce, and Popsicles are not great for your cherished chairs and sofas. Thank goodness for

For a small space—this room is only fifteen feet wide—matching the slipcovers to the white wall and trim makes the room seem bigger. The yellow wall, whose windows let in morning light, gives the room a sunny look.

Brandon's Style Secrets

Slipcovers are a perfect idea for a beach or lake house, where there will be lots of kids and pets. Choose a wash-and-wear fabric to make the slipcovers and make a couple of pairs, so that you can change them out occasionally to change your look. It never hurts to have a holiday set of slipcovers for those big Christmas get-togethers, too.

Slipcover a formal dining chair to give it a more casual feel, or add monograms to your slipcovers for a more upscale look.

Don't be afraid to slipcover other pieces of furniture besides chairs, too. An old table can be inexpensively slipcovered, and topped with a piece of glass to create an entirely new piece of furniture.

Remember, slipcovers are a cheaper way to change the look of furniture than buying new or reupholstering.

waterproof fabrics like Sunbrella that Jane Coslick uses for the slipcovered furniture in all her brightly colored Tybee Island rental cottages. Jane told me that she has thrown those slipcovers in the wash more than one hundred times and they still look great, and the colors stay as bright as new.

I see a lot of off-white slipcovers used in formal dining rooms, and the wonder-

Everything in Jane Coslick's little cottage, above, is a flea market find. The vintage chintz she used for the slipcovers is a design by Carleton Varney, which she found for a song. The chairs are recycled corduroy oldies underneath this fancy dressing.

The slipcovered chairs, at right, disappear into the neutral colors of the wall and banquette seat, letting the artwork and lighting be the focal point of this pretty kitchen table.

ful aspect of off-white chair covers is that you can decorate the table for any holiday or occasion, and use any tablecloth pattern or color of tableware. You don't need to worry about the chairs not matching. The off-white covers frame the table and brighten an otherwise dark room.

Slipcovers hide a multitude of sins and accidents, and that's why Savannahians love them and you will, too.

Sleeping Porches

Years ago, you would find sleepin' porches all over the South. There was no air-conditioning, of course, and indoor rooms could get really sweltering in the dead of summer. People built porches to catch a good breeze, screened them in, and pushed any ol' cot or twin bed outside to brave the elements.

It wasn't just beach houses that had the sleeping porches, either. I've seen lots of mountain cabins that had a pile of single beds out on a screened-in porch, so that all the kids could sleep out there. And, boy, did we kids like sleepin' on the porch! You could talk all night and not bother anyone but the owls. The breezes were cool, and the rustling of the trees was just perfect to help you drift off to dreamland, if you were so inclined.

You do know what old-timey air-conditioning was, don't you? You would put a bowl of ice in front of a fan, place it at the foot of your bed, and it would keep you cool all night, or at least until the ice melted. And you always hoped you'd gone to sleep before it had melted! My eyes are beginning to droop right now.

My husband, Michael, grew up on Wilmington Island right here in Savannah, in a two-bedroom house. He had two

These old fans can be found everywhere these days and I love 'em. There are also new styles that look old and can be mounted on the wall instead of taking up floor space. And there's always the big upright fans—kids love how it sounds to stand in front of one and talk into the rush of air. A summer home in Savannah is not complete without a fan of some sort, even if it is low-tech.

THE ROOST

This sleeping porch started life as a ticket booth for the railroad that brought visitors to Tybee early last century. The single beds were made with local driftwood by a junk collector, Charlie Ellis, and Jane got them at a garage sale.

brothers and the boys all had to share the second bedroom with their grandfather, who lived with them. As soon as it got warm enough to sleep outside, the older boys, Hank and Michael, moved out onto the two single beds on the sleepin' porch. They loved the cool breezes and peein' off the porch, Michael says! In a good year, they could sleep out there six to eight months.

Tybee Island has a lot of lovely old renovated beach cottages. The best ones have been decorated and redone by Jane Coslick, and many of her little beach gems have sleeping porches. She learned the value of this extra space when she was decorating cottages that had only a few hundred square feet of space. Jane was smart to realize that a screened-in porch may be too hot to enjoy during our blazin' hot summer days, but at night it adds a whole other bedroom to your house. After all, you never know what friends might

This Tybee raised cottage was saved from demolition and qualified for designation on the National Register of Historic Places. Raised cottages are in peril because so many were in disrepair and destroyed, and they are now on the endangered list. Diane Kauffman owns this one and rents it out as part of her successful Tybee business, Mermaid Cottages. She collects antique wicker to use in all her beach homes.

A large outside room, screened on two sides, serves as both a sleeping porch and a dining room, depending on the time of day. Decorated with vintage fabrics and furniture, the room is a teen's dream: it's pretty and private!

drop in for a weekend visit, or who the kids might bring home for a sleepover.

Jane's houses have a signature look to them. Not only are they all painted in bright, beachy colors, with fun fabrics and hand-painted signs and local art to match, but they have a retro feel to them that brings up all my good memories of summertime when I was a kid.

Another great sleeping porch of the inland type is the one at the Morrisons' Lebanon Plantation. Of course, plantation houses would always have a lot of wraparound porches, sleeping porches, and such, because when people came to visit they usually stayed awhile. In the old days, when the plantation house was built, the porches were always used in the summer for sleeping. Nowadays, the sleeping porch at Lebanon Plantation is set up as a child's room, and is usually strewn with toys and games. When the sun goes down, the porch is dark enough for the children's bedtime, and the adults can enjoy a few child-free hours before their own bedtime. The more I learn about these old Southern houses, the more I think they got it just right!

Double doors open into the main house and a screen door leads onto an outer porch from the little sleeping porch at Lebanon Plantation. This room is for the grandchildren: close enough to the family to feel safe, and far enough away to seem adventurous.

Brandon's Style Secrets

The first thing to know if you want to create a sleeping porch is don't put the bed on the front porch! Privacy is important and there's more of that on a back or side porch. You can turn a screened porch into a sleeping porch just for a night if you have a bed you can move outside easily. It's a great way to enjoy summer nights or crisp fall weather.

If you don't have a screened porch, consider using mosquito netting over the bed to keep the bugs away. If your local stores don't carry mosquito netting, it's easy to find on the Internet and it's easy to hang. This is an adventure—have fun!

You don't need a fancy bed on your sleeping porch. Find an old bed at a garage sale and repaint it or leave it distressed. Your money will be better spent on good linens to dress it up. Real linen sheets are perfect for a summer night, and you'll never regret the expense.

Tybee Colors

Nothin' cheers me like bright colors, and you can always find the best and the brightest at Tybee. I like color. It makes me happy, and Jane Coslick's little cottages are guaranteed to keep me smiling.

It's funny, isn't it, that something as simple as bright-colored, hand-painted fish and flowers can lift us right up out of the blues? You know, people much smarter than me have written about emotion being tied to color—when we're down we're "blue"; when we feel good we're "in the pink." If you had to put a color to someone with a sunny disposition, you'd say that their color was yellow, wouldn't you?

We all react to bright colors because they seem festive and childlike at the same time. I'm sure that the hand-painted fish on the risers of the steps on the cottage at right would make the trip up to bed a happy one for most kids. The Tybee colors have made their way into stores and restaurants on the island, too. Sometimes when I'm there, I look around me and think I'm on a Caribbean island instead of little old Tybee. If you see me there sipping a rum drink with them tiny umbrellas, remind me I'm not on vacation, okay?

Jane Coslick bought the little cottage, above, in 1998. It was in a blighted condition, but she persisted in telling friends that she would renovate it and get it on the cover of a lifestyle magazine. Most laughed at the idea, but it made the cover of Coastal Living *in January 2000. Jane chose bright colors for this first renovation and the pink color was inspired by a native summer beach flower.*

Brightly painted steps by owner Cindy Hanks lead up to a loft bedroom for kids. Painting the staircase in this way must have been an inspired plan to get them to go to bed after a lively day at the beach!

Brandon's Style Secrets

This look is whimsical and bold. The mix of colors and fabrics creates a bright, youthful style. Nothing is new, but the furniture is not necessarily old, either. Rather, this cottagey look is achieved using furniture with simple, clean lines.

Instead of throwing out that old chest of drawers you've had since college, add odd knobs and paint it an outrageous color. It will add a touch of whimsy to your rooms. Carry the theme throughout with colorful pillows, and a wide mix of colors and patterns in the fabrics. Let your fabrics have a bit of summer fun!

Go wild with painted details—bright-colored doors, staircases, sills, and furniture can have a new life as a cheerful beach cottage.

What has become a signature Tybee style, bright colors and mixed fabric patterns are a cheerful way to bring the colors of summer into a home. Anything goes in color combinations in Tybee cottages, and the bedside table scene at left is a testament to color courage that works. I like the little fish drawer pulls that brighten up an otherwise plain bedside table.

She Sells Seashells

You can't live near the beach without being a shell-hound. We are sittin' smack in the middle of the Low Country, which is mostly marshes and creeks. All of these creeks are crusted with oyster beds, so you see oyster shells everywhere. Not everyone would think to collect oyster shells rather than seashells, but Kathy Jarman does. She collects all sorts of shells, actually, then she does amazing things with them.

Used to be that souvenir shops on beaches around the country would be filled with kitschy little things made out of seashells. It kind of gave shelling a bad name, I'm afraid. Since this book is all about Savannah style, I wanted to introduce you to some seriously unique objects and people. Kathy Jarman creates shell artwork that's more than the souvenir objects we're used to finding in coastal towns. She covers whole sideboards with shells; patterns whole bathroom walls with them; covers lamp bases, sculpts busts, and decorates tables with them. The plain old oyster shell becomes something really stylish in Kathy's hands.

I've always collected shells. You'd be weird if you didn't want to gather shells

Artist and designer Kathy Jarman's house is a gallery of her fabulous shell art. The oyster-shell lamp bases, Poseidon sculpture, and shell-encrusted cornice board work together to match the sophisticated neutral color scheme.

when you are living on the water and visiting the beach as often as we do in Savannah. Most everyone I know has a bowl full of shells on one of their tables. Shells remind us of great times we've spent doing nothin' but kicking along the sand, looking at our toes, searching for treasure. It's the scavenger, or the treasure hunter, in me that likes to bring home pretty things I've found and make them into something even more wonderful.

Another local designer makes oyster-shell chandeliers that are turning up on porches and in dining rooms all over town. I like flea markets for the same reason. Whatever you collect, you can usually find great bargains and fun things to add to your collection at auctions and flea markets at a fraction of

Kathy's Welsh dresser–style buffet is encrusted with shells in repeating patterns, with mirrored countertops that reflect this fantasy wonderland of shells. Appropriately, the buffet holds Kathy's large collection of fish plates.

The two busts, right, were garage sale finds that Kathy painted and artfully decorated with shells, coral, and semiprecious stones. These ladies look like they are deep-sea royalty!

the price of buying it new. I'm a great lover of flea markets and I'll talk more about those later.

If Kathy's things make you want to go right out and buy a glue gun just so you can prettify your old sideboard, you're not the only one. But if you're like me, and don't have a crafty bone in your body, then you can always find creative ways to display your best shells. My friend Jeannie Sims shows off her shells in her pretty antique silver epergne, which makes a wonderful table centerpiece for a summer party.

There are a thousand ways to display shells, either as rotating collectibles or as a permanent part of your decor.

Jeannie Sims likes to fill her silver and crystal epergne, upper left, with her loveliest shells for a natural centerpiece to her summer party table.

A local artist makes popular chandeliers out of strands of oyster shells, like this one, upper right.

Brandon's grouping of three impressively large pieces of coral add a year-round botanical look to a fireplace mantel in his parlor.

Brandon's Style Secrets

No matter where you live, shells add a chic and pretty element to any tabletop arrangement, centerpiece, or collection display. If you've ever visited a beach, you have a reason to collect shells. Of course, today you can buy wonderful shells from a variety of places to add to or start a collection.

The key to a collection of beautiful shells is how you display them. Use them with silver and crystal bowls for an elegant centerpiece for your next dinner party. Display a few large shells or pieces of coral along a mantelpiece.

If you really love shells, look for the many ways they are used in home decor these days. Don't be afraid to hang a quirky oyster-shell chandelier in your dining room, kitchen, or on a porch.

Southerners are good at finding different uses for everyday objects. For instance, we use tabby—an old Low Country building material made of lime, sand, and oyster shells—for our walkways, fireplaces, and garden walls. We cover furniture, walls, mirrors, and jewelry with shells. Don't be afraid to take an antique piece and cover it with a shell design. I say, use the hell out of your shells! They give any room an organic feel.

Cool Parlors

Ever heard of the faintin' couch? It was not just a Southern myth that nineteenth-century women needed them for that purpose, you know. And, believe me, women didn't used to faint just because their stays were too tight! No sir, it was the heat in the South (plus all those petticoats) that caused women to feel faint in the heat of the day. That's why the faintin' couch came in handy. Brandon tells me it's called something far more elegant, but I just can't ever pronounce "chaise" right, and it's entirely too French-soundin', anyway.

In Savannah, we still love a room that is a retreat from the summer heat. These rooms are usually located on the parlor floor, which in the historic town houses is the first floor up a flight of stairs. Because our town houses have windows mainly at the front and back of the houses (unless it has a side garden, it shares its two long walls with the town houses on either side), the rooms can be kept cool and dark in the midday summer heat by simply drawing the curtains or shades. Savannahians decorate parlor rooms to look and feel cool by using colors and fabrics that are simple, without busy patterns or overly fussy

Carolyn Hultman's peach and pale gold color scheme is feminine, cool, and calm. She uses flowers and her collection of porcelain fruits to infuse small spots of brighter color.

Carolyn bought the chaise, at right, when she moved to Savannah. She says she wanted to be Southern in the worst way! When she removed the wall between the dining room and parlor, she added wooden Corinthian columns for support.

Everything in Carolyn Hultman's parlor is inviting and relaxing, thanks to her color scheme and the simplicity of the decor.

Jeannie Sims's parlor is only fifteen feet wide, but it is inviting and simple in its design. The neutral colors with the additions of silver ornaments and a little round aluminum table, mirrored tabletop, and fireplace surround add sparkle to the room.

Although this historic town house is traditional in design, Jeannie's rooms feel contemporary and new. The old Chippendale sofa has been slipcovered in a soft, ultrasuede fabric to give it a more modern look.

Brandon's Style Secrets

In Savannah, the parlor is traditionally the show-stopping room of the house. We put all our money into making the parlor beautiful. Our old historic homes have gigantic parlors, often with multiple fireplaces and room for a large dining table.

Large rooms call for more pieces, so the key to a look that is calm, not busy, is to stick to neutral colors—tone-on-tone, or cool colors.

Cool fabrics add to the comfort of any room. Choose linens, cottons, or silks for upholstery, drapery, and pillows. Steer away from nubby textures.

Choose monochromatic flower arrangements like cream roses in small bunches to place on your tables.

Keep the lighting dim and cool. Try to balance the light in the room by using the same amount of wattage for ceiling light as you use in your floor lamps. Add up those amps and equalize the amount you use, and you'll feel the difference. Don't be afraid to use a lower amp bulb.

The Parkers' parlor has French influences and, except for the carpet, is almost atonal in color. The double chandeliers are reflected in all of the three large mirrors, and just fills the room with light. Notice the conversational grouping of comfortable chairs with a reading table, near the front of the room overlooking the street. This is a multiuse room that makes the most of its length. The curtained side doors at left lead onto a side porch, so this room has a good deal of traffic. It isn't one of those unused living rooms.

details. Sometimes, the only strong colors you'll see in a parlor are the seasonal flowers on display.

Jeannie Sims's parlor just oozes calmness with its silver and off-white color scheme. Every little thing she puts in her parlor is chosen for its pale color or reflective quality, and the result is a busy room that nonetheless is soothing and inviting. Even the painting of a palm tree over the mantel adds to the overall feeling; you can almost hear the breeze rustling the fronds on a hot afternoon.

Ellen Bolch has taken the silvery theme a step further in her riverfront house by using silver foil on her walls, and painting the mantelpiece a weathered gray that blends well with the wall color. An arched doorway opens into a small, mirrored bar space off this beautiful parlor, and I just know that everyone gathers here at cocktail hour in the summer to have that first gin and tonic.

The Parkers' sophisticated parlor on

The Bolches' Federal-style settee, above, was redone in colors to complement the silk drapery, and Ellen used the actual drapery fabric in small inset panels on the sides of the cushions. The Corinthian reproduction urn holds an impressive spray of orchids, which are all the rage in Savannah homes.

The Bolches' parlor, opposite, features blocked wallpaper of a silvery metallic color. The oversize Venetian mirror adds another layer to the silver walls, and a little bar tucked in the small hallway between two rooms is also mirrored. Adding the bar is an example of a great use of space—in this case, a passageway between two rooms—that would otherwise have been overlooked.

Gaston Street in the historic district is another great example of a color palette used to its best effect. The pale yellows reflect light from the windows, and the room exudes a pale sunlit quality even when the drapes are drawn.

I wouldn't be a good momma if I didn't tell you about my son Bobby's parlor. He would tell you, though, that it's his party room or his video room, not a parlor! But with a very masculine decor, and dark curtains that can block out any light, it is "cool" in every sense of the word. Bobby uses this room as a projection room, too. The screen drops down from the ceiling when he wants to view movies with friends, and the many areas of seating make for a very comfortable room.

Brandon designed this room for Bobby, and it includes a bar from Bobbie Gentry's studio office in Los Angeles, a large rectangular opium table that works as a coffee table, heavy-gauge curtains to block out the light, and enough seating for a crowd of twelve to sixteen guests.

Bobby fell in love with the turtle shells I display on the table in my foyer, so for his birthday the year he bought this house, I gave him the big turtle shell that is mounted over his fireplace.

Bobby Deen's parlor doubles as a media room where he can entertain friends in grand style. A large screen lowers from one of the faux rafters. This room's sophisticated bachelor appeal suits him perfectly.

Family Memories

I never will forget the time Michael and my kids all got together to surprise me with the engagement ring that Michael had bought for me. And I won't have to worry about forgetting, because I keep the picture of me with my mouth open in surprise right on my "memory table." I can relive all those sweet emotions every time I look at it. I know, there's nothin' new under the sun about collecting family photos. Everyone has 'em, but at my house we treat them like our best treasures. When you have a big family, it's important that every one of them see their picture in a pretty frame, sitting in a place of importance when they visit. The fact that they know I am always thinkin' of them when I'm home is part of the glue that sticks us together. It doesn't hurt that I keep some of my photos of me with the celebrities I've met right beside the everyday shots of my brother, my uncles, kids, dogs, nephews, and nieces. Makes them feel good, too.

Now, you might think I'm a little crazy to frame pictures of my dogs, but I told you early on that Savannah's very accepting of eccentricity. Otis and Sam are my oldest, and they get the lead dog positions on my bedside table!

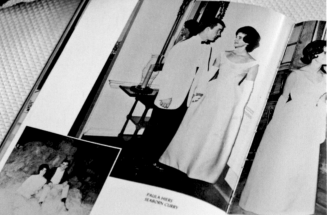

This old yearbook, above, is open to my "Senior Superlative" portrait from high school. Our senior class chose ten students who were the most popular to be the "Senior Superlative" students. I had a lot of fun in high school and I guess I was a popular cutup!

Autumn

I don't know about y'all, but autumn

really gets my juices flowing. It must be the cool air, such a pick-me-up after the dog days of summer. Seein' pumpkins on every stoop and front porch puts a smile on my face because it reminds me of Halloween and all the fun the children have on that night—not to mention all the candy. Y'all know what a weakness I have for candy.

More than that, fall means a time for having friends and family over. Whether it's holiday get-togethers, dinners, or football parties, I know it's time to start sprucing up my house for company.

In Savannah, we like to dress up the front of our homes for the season, and this means putting out the pumpkins as soon as we can get our hands on them. We welcome autumn, because it's a relief from the dog days of summer.

The lovely old Ballastone Inn, at left, doesn't stop with one pumpkin. These remind me of a string of beads, placed along the stairway.

The Foltz family's suburban Savannah porch is a fall festival of cornstalks, garden mums, pumpkins, bittersweet, Indian corn, and fall leaves. What a treat for the eyes!

Y'all Come On In!

First impressions matter, as my daddy used to say. I never left our house without him reminding me that I had one chance to make a good impression that day. I had to put my best foot forward if I wanted to get ahead, and that piece of good advice has done me a world of good throughout my life. Bless you, Daddy!

When there's a guest comin' to my house—and believe me, we have family and friends over all the time—I always make sure that my front hallway is picture-perfect, clean and pretty. It says a lot about my house that the first image a visitor has is of a neat, colorful, table with a few cherished objects, some fabulous seasonal flowers that Brandon has usually cut and done up for me, and my collection of walking canes by the door. The view of my living room beyond is part of the picture, to be sure, but that first impression has to be a good one: it's an invitation to come on in.

The foyer at my house at Turner's Creek is about the same length as the width of my front porch, and its plank walls are similar to the outside walls of the house. When you open my big ol' double screen doors and step inside, the entranceway gives the feelin' that you're

The Lindleys' marble-topped table, above, holds an impressive array of fresh seasonal flowers, which gives a great first impression.

My foyer, opposite, is an extension of my porch, with its painted wood walls. *I put lots of my favorite things in the foyer, such as my walking stick collection, my turtle shells, a bunch of flowers from my garden, and one of my favorite pieces, a farmhouse table that dates from about 1910.*

Brandon's Style Secrets

Foyers set the tone of your home; it's a preview of what's to come. Your front hallway should match the rest of your house in style and mood. I like to think of the foyer as a small still life of the entire house.

The size of your space doesn't matter—drama is what's important. Be careful when choosing the furniture you put in a foyer; it's the place to put your star pieces. Many people feel that a good piece will be overlooked in a room that guests just walk through, but actually the opposite is true. A great piece of furniture or a wonderful mirror will create a lasting impression.

Don't hesitate to use and display a variety of things in a foyer: flower arrangements, large-scale mirrors and art, murals, gold- or silver-leaved ceiling details. Chandeliers are great in a small space. Step out of the box and layer elements.

Keep in mind that this is not just a room to hang your coat. It's not just a pass-through space. I like to think of a foyer as the handbag for a new outfit!

not really inside the house at that point. Usually the dogs are jumpin' all over you wantin' to be petted, and there may be coats to be hung up and packages to be set aside on the table. That foyer serves a lot of purposes, but goin' back to my daddy's advice, the best thing it does is set a good impression.

The rows of historic town houses in downtown Savannah usually open right onto a hallway that runs the length of the house, so a guest has a view of the main stairway and a little glimpse into the rooms that connect onto the hallway on one side. There are some Federal-style town houses that are wide enough to have rooms on either side of the hallway, but the front doors always open onto the hallway, even in these. In this case, it's important that the hallway is inviting and well maintained. Hallways are usually the forgotten room in a house, but I like 'em because they're usually where people put the family portraits. You can see the whole history of the person in that little space.

Southern hosts still keep to the tradition of placing a table by the front door. In the old days, people might leave their calling cards on a little silver tray set on this table. These days, entranceway tables are a great place to decorate with seasonal greens and arrangements of flowers. But even now, you can usually be sure that the mail will find its way to this table, too. I always drop my mail on the hallway table, especially if it's bills!

The foyer at Lebanon Plantation isn't large, but it is impressive. The one-of-a-kind hall table with mirror, purchased at auction, had to be slightly altered to fit the height of the room. Bob Christian painted a special faux arbor to frame the piece.

Comfort Rooms

I grew up with the notion that living rooms had to have furniture "sets"—all matching and bought at the same time. That's what people did in Albany, Georgia, and pretty much all over the South if you weren't rich or hadn't inherited antiques.

The livin' room was always the "good room" in the house where guests were entertained, but the family rarely used it the rest of the time, except maybe when the relatives all came for the holidays. The kids pretty much kept out of it, because if Momma's couch was stained by dirty hands, or the rug had muddy shoe prints, we were in a lot of trouble. The livin' room was not a comfortable room in my childhood experience.

Thank the Lord that's changed these days. Now livin' rooms are for livin'! I keep enough chairs and couches in mine to seat an army, and the dogs can hop on up anytime they want to. I like a casual livin' room, and ours opens up right onto the creek out back. I can hear the boats comin' before I see them putter by, and I can hear the marsh birds. I don't feel shut up in the house, even when the windows are closed. That makes the livin' room a comfort room for me, because I never forget that I'm on the water that I love so much.

And my livin' room has lots of my favorite things in it, including Michael's captain's wheel that I surprised him with on his birthday one year. Not your usual livin' room decoration, but we both love it and I can't imagine it anywhere else in our house.

The simple corner, below, has all that you need for a comfortable reading space—lots of light . . . and no clutter.

Carolyn Hultman's
Asian-inspired dining room also
serves as a library and reading
room when not used for
dinner parties.

Brandon's Style Secrets

A comfort room should feel informal rather than formal. In Savannah, that means it has a more worn look (or some artful fakery) acquired through years of loving use.

Books and treasures you display should be within arm's reach. Clean up the clutter of collections by clustering your prized possessions, and frequently rotating them so that you don't show them all at once.

Lighting and seating are both equally important to your feeling of comfort. Do you want the room for reading or for conversation? Use lighting that reflects your needs.

Even a formal room design must put people at ease to be a successful space. Use pillows, pillows, and more pillows! Warm, rich colors work well.

A fireplace can be the focal point of a room. Don't be afraid to use the comfort of a fireplace to make a formal room seem more inviting.

If the room comes with a view, let that be the focal point of the room. Don't hang big art or use tall pieces to overwhelm the beauty of the natural view. Make sure the view can be enjoyed either sitting or standing.

If you have rugs, use them! The more, the better. Layering is key to comfort.

I love my casually elegant living room, which looks out onto Turner's Creek. There's nothing on the walls to impede the view of the water. The simple colors and matching furniture are all designed to play second fiddle to the view.

Paula Danyluk, who owns The Paris Market, uses fall colors on pillows and furniture grouped around a big fireplace to create a cozy living room. The black-and-white photos on the wall are vacation travel photos she's taken and then framed.

Because I was frustrated that I couldn't always find the kind of furniture pieces that I wanted, I've designed my own, which have become part of the Paula Deen Home Collection. When I started thinkin' what I wanted for my very own furniture designs, I wanted the pieces not to look like they came out of a furniture store. When we buy a chair or table for our home, we want each piece to tell a story of who we are. That's the kind of special that I want in my furniture. Everyone's idea of what makes a room comfortable is different, as it should be, but in Savannah the one common thread is that people like to see and be seen. It's not hard to be seen in Savannah, even if you're inside. The older homes are situated close to the street, and there's usually a little table set close to a window that gives out onto a view of the front garden and the busy sidewalk.

Of course, a comfort room need not be your living room. Lots of Savannahians use their big, round dining tables for reading tables instead of, or in addition to, serving food. My friend Carolyn Hultman does this because she likes to eat out a lot. Sometimes she stacks loads of her favorite books on her big round table, and it just draws you to it, and you invariably want to sit down and read. She's created a comfort room for both herself and her guests.

Music Rooms

I can't play a lick on any instrument, but I've decided to buy me a piano anyway. I have a couple of great friends who can play the heck out of it, so I'm gonna get one for the livin' room. We've decided to get a player piano so that we can "play" it even if the friends aren't here to serenade us.

My momma insisted that I take piano lessons when I was little. My teacher's name was Mrs. Bland, and she taught me first to play using numbers that indicated which keys to press. She stuck little numbers on the keys of the piano. I was doin' fine there for a while, but when she graduated me to reading notes instead of numbers, I was totally confused, so that was the end of my musical career.

If you play an instrument, you never think twice about makin' room for it in your house. There will just naturally be a room that's your music room. It can be just a small corner of the livin' room if you don't have a whole room to devote to music.

In the genteel homes of the old South, people entertained at home, and played music for their guests. This was true all over the country, I guess, not just in the South. A talented guest might be ex-

pected to "sing for their supper." It was common for the women in the family to be schooled in music; in fact, it was a sign of good breeding. Frankly, I'm still impressed with anyone who has musical talent. Brandon is a wonderful pianist. He'll be one of the first people I invite to play my new piano, you can be sure of that.

Musical instruments are beautiful pieces of furniture in their own right. Early 1900s engravings, found at a flea market and simply framed, are an inexpensive, elegant addition to the black and white room.

Going Formal

Jim Williams was the infamous person who convinced Savannah to give formal parties again. You may have read about him in John Berendt's famous book *Midnight in the Garden of Good and Evil*. He threw lavish formal dinners and entertained throughout the 1970s and '80s at a level that locals hadn't experienced since before the Civil War. The people in this city were offended if they weren't invited to his famous holiday parties, and everyone coveted an invitation. The rest of his life was tragic, and the book is a wonderful story of the murder for which he was tried and acquitted, but Savannah has not forgotten his love of formal dining.

I will admit this right now: my least favorite thing to do is to sit at a formal table or to give a formal dinner. It's just not my style. Brandon likes to give big formal dinners, and he has a house that's perfect for them—it's a big old Victorian that he restored, using dark colors, lots of wood, and oversize chandeliers in many of the rooms, including the kitchen. The result is a mix of antique and modern styles that is totally New South—and also drop-dead gorgeous!

His big ol' dining table always seems to be set for twelve people, and when he's

Brandon's oversize chandelier hangs low over his large dining table, creating an intimate table atmosphere that brings the eye down from the high ceilings. Brandon regularly throws dinner parties for twelve, so he likes to do small multiple flower arrangements and spread them down the length of his table. The guests all feel that the flowers are just for them, and the multiple bunches make the table even more beautiful.

home, he's usually cooking for that many guests. I figure I must have rubbed off on him; he loves to entertain! Of course, throwing a dinner party is a very popular pastime in Savannah, so as you can imagine, there are more than a few elegant, formal dining rooms around town.

Of course, a formal dining table isn't just for big dinner parties. If you want what I call a "romantical" dinner, then a table set for two in a beautiful dining room can create the right mood for romance. Using a beautiful tablecloth, your fine china, silver, and crystal is the perfect way to let that certain someone know they're special.

When I catered parties, I had the chance to see inside a lot of wonderful old homes with fancy dining tables, many having been passed down from generation to generation. The best of these dining rooms always seemed to include a good mix of old and new things. For example, combining an antique table with modern upholstered chairs with simple lines can be more comfy than using some of the antique chairs of the same period. And the result can be a more modern look for the dining room.

If you have a collection of art to show off, there's no better place to hang it than in the dining room. When everyone is seated at the table, you've got a captive audience, and if the conversation falters, you can always talk about the art.

Again, as with the furniture, mixing

The Lindleys' art collection is extensive, but they particularly like the work of local artists, so the place of honor in their dining room features one of Laura DiNello's unique mosaic paintings. Two beautiful family portraits (by W. Parker Beach) can be seen from the table.

The Danyluks' dining room is a traditional delight. The table and chairs are the stars, and the chandelier is a sparkling and elegant antique. I like the way the flowers make a room look lived-in, whether or not it's in use at the moment.

family portraits with your favorite modern art make for good company on your dining room walls. The Lindleys' renovated Victorian on the Isle of Hope in Savannah is a great example of mixing lovely antiques with exciting new art. They have a large collection, made larger with the paintings and drawings they've inherited over the years. The eye-catching mosaic that hangs over their dining room sideboard is by a local artist. Although their tastes at first seem eclectic, most of the paintings on display are by local artists. You can gather from the many family portraits that the appreciation of painting and collecting art is part of their Savannah family heritage.

The other thing that we all love to add to a formal dinner table is a big vase of fresh flowers. Sure, there are lots of creative and entertaining centerpieces that you can do for a seasonal table setting, but the one sure thing that is always beautiful is to choose and cut the prettiest, freshest flowers you can find and let those be your centerpiece for a special dinner party.

There is no one who understands this more than Brandon, who keeps amazing me with his colorful arrangements, both big and small. Flowers are a way to bring color into any room, and are a focal point for a table with the right color and size. And Savannahians don't decorate a table just for a party. Dressing the table with beautiful flowers keeps a room alive, even when no one is sitting at the table.

Brandon's Style Secrets

Practically every historic home in Savannah has a formal dining room. We love our parties and we love to decorate a table.

An antique dining table gives a good first impression, but you can get a more contemporary look by using slipcovers on the chairs. Don't be afraid to break tradition—there are no rules to creating a formal dining room. It's okay to mix old and new pieces in new, quirky ways.

Your table and chairs are the stars of this room. The chandelier is the second most important item; it is the sparkling engagement ring for the room.

Dare to be different. Paint the ceiling a bold color, or use a bold wallpaper design.

Dramatize the room with flowers in any season. Don't be afraid to use small bunches of blooms to line a tabletop instead of one big arrangement. Anything goes!

When you're not entertaining, a big bowl of flowers or fruit on your table keeps the room alive and inviting.

Add a touch of whimsy to your dining room by draping a chandelier with tulle for a party or a holiday get-together. Little touches are sometimes the ones we remember the most.

Book Nooks

I raised my boys to love to read and told them they'd never regret it, and Momma was right. Now they have their own books—literally! Their first two books are both successful, and you can bet they're happy their old momma taught them to love to read.

My son Jamie remodeled his house in 2008, adding two rooms and a library. Jamie is just wild about books, and he says he likes to go in there by himself, grab a book, and be alone with his thoughts. That's pure happiness for him. Some of his books came from Grandmother and Granddaddy Paul's Magnolia Lodge, a hunting and fishing lodge full of antiques and books that they had for years. Jamie always coveted those books, and now he has some in his own library.

A library seems like a private room to me, but that doesn't mean it shouldn't be well designed and inviting. A roomful of books tells a guest a good bit about the person who lives there. Haven't you ever taken a close look at a friend's bookshelf just to see what they're reading lately? Come on now, admit it!

Libraries and smaller bookshelf areas—I'll call them book nooks—can be

Who says you can't have fun in a library? Both these rooms feature fun details. Below, the bookshelf doors are faced with chicken wire rather than glass.

In the Bolches' library, opposite, wallpaper with a book motif is mixed with shelves of real books. The dog portrait by local painter Troy Wandzel hangs on a wallpapered wall. When I'm in this room, I just want to kick off my shoes and get comfy with a good book!

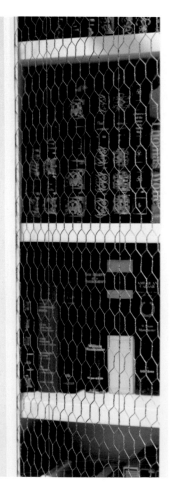

Brandon's Style Secrets

A library doesn't need to be a room. You can create one in a pass-through hallway, or by adding shelves under a stairway—spaces that are not normally used.

Remember, a library is not just for books. It is a great place to display your treasures. Artwork, collectibles, and family portraits will personalize this space.

Take a tip from bookstores and display some of your more beautiful books face out, rather than spine out. They become a conversation piece and a focal point of the space that way.

easy to design and decorate. After all, the books themselves are the main decoration. Either covering the walls or just tucked up under the stairs in a handful of shelves, books are a fun way to tell people who we are.

The two book nooks on this page are great examples of space that might otherwise go unused.

The bookshelves at the stairway landing come complete with a window seat for browsing. And the shelves inset under a stairway afford a great place to display books and objects.

Jamie Deen's library is a reading room as well as an office. Many of his books are saved from childhood and his great-grandmother's family retreat that holds fond memories for him. A library can, and should, be a very personal space.

Collecting

I don't know if collecting is a national pastime, but Southerners do spend an inordinate amount of time amassing things they love. There's not a house in Savannah that doesn't lovingly display a collection of silver, plates, pottery, canes, ceramics, crafts, or anything that takes our fancy. Sometimes we start collecting because we have a couple of pieces handed down to us from our family that we cherish and we want to have more of them. Sometimes we find something unique, like the abstract designs of African plates and bowls woven out of colored wire that Kathy Jarman displays on a hallway bench.

My good friend designer Carolyn Hultman creates clever little compositions on her mantelpiece with her paintings of fruit and the ceramic fruits that she collects. They change from season to season, and I look to see what's new whenever I visit her.

The traditional collectible for Southerners is silver, and I'll talk more about that in the next chapter—collecting antique silver is almost a religion for Southerners. Occasionally, though, I see silver collections that are offbeat and fun, like Charlie Brown's tray of loving cups. He acquired them at auction

The sterling trophies, below, are part of silver expert Charlie Brown's collection, and each has a touch of whimsy. The small Tiffany trophy in the foreground was awarded to the Carswell family of Augusta for being the perfect hosts. Another trophy is titled "The James Day Trophy for Amateurs."

Displaying your collection is not rocket science, but it does take some imagination to do well. Finding the perfect spot, grouping the items so they show well, and treating your collectibles as things that should be used and shown off is key. If you love your collectibles, you want others to recognize their worth, too.

Two collections are usually on display at my house. The tea set, at top, was purchased intact from a local dealer. Below is my Grandmother Paul's collection of cranberry glasses, which I inherited.

and the inscriptions on them will make you laugh out loud. "For the Perfect Hosts" is inscribed on one cup—it must have originally been an impressive hostess gift!

Everything that I collect seems to be something related to cooking and eating, which is perfect for me, don't you agree? I have a big ol' cabinet in my living room that holds my silver spoons, Grandmother Paul's cranberry glasses, and a few special collectible items. The cranberry glassware is my favorite because it was my grandmomma's originally, but I always like to find more pieces to add to it. Collecting a pattern that has been handed down through generations can be fun and full of good memories each time you use the pieces. What I love most about Savannahians are the creative ways they manage to show off their collections. For those downtown, who have windows that can be seen from the street, the window becomes a stage for some of their collectibles. That group of loving cups could turn up on a dinner table, filled with cut flowers. Or like my canes by the front door, you can display things to be used, picked up, and admired. I imagine that someone who borrowed one of my canes would remember picking it out from all the others, and would be thoughtful about returning it.

Brandon's Style Secrets

The key to displaying a special collection is not to spread it throughout your home. Find a place—a table, a secretary, some bookshelves, or a display cabinet—that is sufficiently big to hold your collection, but not so big as to dwarf it. Think of creative ways to display your collectibles. Don't think you have to have an antique china cabinet to display a collection.

Grouping objects gives them visual value and importance. Use your collection if it's usable. If you don't want the pieces handled, make sure your treasures are behind glass, or tucked inside a cabinet, so that guests need to ask to touch them.

Don't be afraid to collect anything that you love. I love turtles, so I collect turtle shells wherever I travel. Conversely, don't be embarrassed to use the Internet. You don't have to travel these days to add to a collection.

It's okay to mix old and new pieces. Diligent collectors will haunt estate sales and flea markets to find what they want. Follow your heart and look for collectibles anywhere you can.

Silver & Savannahians

You're just not a Southerner if you don't have any silver pieces that are older than your grandmomma. There are dealers who specialize in older pieces with great history (and big prices!) and these exceptional silver pieces grace many a table in the city.

Southerners are very interested in their heritage; there is a great deal of local interest in nineteenth-century silver made and sold here in the South. Most of these pieces are referred to as coin silver and bear hallmarks of Southern silversmiths.

Objects made of silver were an important reflection of the conspicuous consumption practiced by wealthy early Americans, and the Southern elite were particularly fond of the value and beauty of the silversmiths' products.

Records exist of numerous silversmiths working in Savannah during the 1800s. Silversmith shops opened throughout the business district, on Broughton, Whitaker, and Drayton streets. A freedman, Shark Marquand, was even known to own his own silver business.

The Savannah-made silver that survives today is mostly flatware and pieces of tea services.

The child's high chair, above, displays some of the grandchildren's silver pieces. A little nameplate on the front of the chair lists all the grandchildren's names, too.

The fabulous table setting, opposite, looks fit for a queen. All the separate pieces are from Charlie Brown's shop in the historic district, C. H. Brown Fine Silver & Antiques, and include an epergne, circa 1850, from a Savannah estate; Bohemian glass goblets and finger bowl, circa 1840–1860; and Wedgwood china and a sterling goblet from 1792 that belonged to the first mayor of Savannah, Thomas Gibbons.

Probably the most common sight when you enter a historic Savannah home is the silver tea service, usually displayed on a sideboard. If it has not been handed down through generations of the family, then it has been lovingly collected, and you can be sure that the owner will eagerly tell you its history and provenance.

Of course, silver is lovely when paired with other collectibles as part of a display. Even if your silver is not antique, it adds luster and highlights to anything around it. The one thing that I would advise you to do with any of the silver you have is—show it off!

Charlie Brown's shelves, opposite, hold more than silver. They hold history. The two creamware plates are from the 1840s. The shelf below holds various American coin silver goblets and drinking cups, and the tea set below is vintage 1930s American sterling.

I just started collecting silver a few years ago, so my collection is small, but I love to show it off in my armoire in the living room. Above, this little group of silver pieces includes a Victorian biscuit barrel (which can be used on special occasions for dog biscuits!), and an Edwardian creamer and sugar. I mix in my silverplate; it all looks great together.

Rarely do you enter a historic Savannah home that you don't see a sideboard showing off a silver service, either inherited or collected. Of course, the older the silver, the better, but if it isn't your grandmomma's silver, no one minds. The display opposite is the daily setup for breakfast at the Ballastone Inn. Charlie Brown keeps lots of little silver demitasse spoons on hand for the inns to buy, because their stock is often depleted by tourists who want to take a little bit of antique silver home as a souvenir.

Brandon's Style Secrets

Silver can be used for generations without worrying that it might get chipped or broken. It is so popular that collecting silver is almost a Southern pastime. Don't be afraid to mix and match styles and quality of your pieces. If you like a silverplate design, don't be afraid to use it alongside your antique silver.

Silver objects transcend every style of decor. Don't be afraid to use a silver collection to complement both modern and antique furniture.

Silver doesn't need to be polished constantly to be party-ready and beautiful. The old patina of silver is particularly lovely. It shows the age and use of a piece.

Best of all, you can find additions to your silver collection at garage sales, yard sales, antique markets, auctions, estate sales, and all sorts of fun places.

Finally, if you have it, show it off! For a beautiful look, place a bunch of red roses in a silver teapot or wine bucket. Be creative about how you use your silver, but be sure to use it.

Taxidermy

Okay, now, I know what you're thinkin.'
You're thinkin', *un-unh, not Bambi*. Well, it's true, Savannah has a long history of hunters who love to shoot game, stuff it, and hang it on the wall. Hunting is still a popular sport in the South and taxidermy is a very popular collectible, even if you're not a great hunter.

My hometown of Albany was right in the middle of Georgia's quail country and I grew up seeing stuffed quail decorating many homes there. My daddy exposed both my boys to hunting early on, and they decided it wasn't their

The composition of quail, at left, shows the creativity that goes into posing taxidermy to look natural. A cluster of these pieces looks like a real grouping of the Georgia state bird.

Opposite, beautiful and colorful Victorian taxidermy songbirds are perched on a branch, complete with a nest. Preserved under a glass bell, the presentation is typical of popular taxidermy for that time.

The early 1900s vintage taxidermy goat and badger are both from Belgium. Taxidermy is popular not only in the South, as you can see by these European antiques.

sport. Myself, I prefer to keep my birds alive and in a cage!

I've got to admit that the Savannah style of displaying taxidermy is often very creative, and I'm always delighted to visit homes that have tabletop vignettes featuring local specimens, like the quail grouping at Lebanon Plantation.

Even if you don't have a liking for stuffed animals that aren't from a toy store, you can find beautiful compositions under glass—complete with colorful birds and delicate nests—that will please even the faint of heart. Taxidermy is a great addition to a man's office or library, and a longtime staple of Southern style.

Brandon's Style Secrets

In the South, nothing defines a man's style like taxidermy. Savannah takes collecting taxidermy to the next level of decorating.

Taxidermy is not for everyone, but if you need a touch of eclecticism in your life, this is it! Your grandfather or great-grandfather may have been a hunter, even if you aren't. Vintage taxidermy is very popular right now, so don't hesitate to use any old pieces you have.

Finding the right vintage piece is key. If you want to add a touch of whimsy to a home office, what about a little stuffed goat or a badger? The only rule here is to stay away from stuffed dogs or cats. Family pets are just not the right subject matter for displaying taxidermy.

The Victorians popularized the art of creating little vignettes within bell jars, using birds, plants, and butterflies for a more feminine effect. These pretty collectibles may be more to your taste, if you like to add nature specimens to your home.

The Art of Faux

If my darlin' birds saw this painting of exotic caged birds that hangs on Carolyn Hultman's wall, they would think they could talk to them. The local artist and muralist who painted it, Bob Christian, is a real master of the art of illusion. I guess, to a certain extent, all art is illusion, but Bob takes his three-dimensional creations off the canvas, and paints on walls, ceilings, furniture, and floors to delight and surprise the viewer. He can imitate dozens of wood grains and marbles, parquetry, ivory, patterned cloth, as well as creating *faux-ivoire* candlesticks and intricately painted and lacquered rugs made of canvas.

Historically, mural paintings in the old South were a popular adornment for public buildings, like theaters, libraries, and schools. Many of these have been preserved. The most famous one in Georgia has to be the 365-degree wall mural in the Cyclorama and Civil War Museum in Atlanta, depicting the Battle of Atlanta. Every Georgia schoolchild has either seen it or seen pictures of it.

Murals depicting the gentility of life in the South are popular around Savannah, in private homes and in some

When Carolyn remodeled her home, she saw that she had mismatched wood where the walls once were—the floorboards were laid in different directions. Using faux detailing, she had the floorboards painted to look like inlaid parquetry.

The same artist, Bob Christian, painted the birdcage that hangs on the wall of Carolyn's in-kitchen dining room. You'd swear you could hear these birds sing in the morning!

of the bed-and-breakfast inns, too. Faux wall details, ceiling paintings that bring to mind European churches, and even the occasional exterior wall painting of climbing vines or flowering potted plants can be seen around town. I always do a double take when I notice one of these little eye-teasers. I like people who decorate with a sense of humor!

Southerners take great stock in the beauty of things, and Greg and Kelly Parker's dining room mural of terraced balconies amid a gracious garden is the best example of this that I can recall. It created a calm, beautiful space that was instantly pleasant and relaxing. Lit by a floor-to-ceiling window on the north side of the house, the changing light added drama to the room.

Faux wall painting and detailing has been popular now for a couple of decades and you can find examples of it all over the city, in even the most humble of places. I recently noticed a group of student apartments downtown—many students from the Savannah College of Art and Design live in this area—that had paintings of potted plants alongside the doorways. For these enterprising art students, it was a great way to create their own garden, and it makes everyone who sees it smile.

A clever trompe l'oeil composition of bricks and a potted plant dresses up an otherwise plain downtown apartment entranceway. We are a town full of art students, so it's not unusual to discover this sort of creativity on every corner.

The elegant mural opposite is all this dining room needs to dress it up. The multidimensional subject matter fools the eye into thinking the room is bigger than it really is.

Brandon's Style Secrets

If you don't own an old home, you can get the same look with faux finishes. They are a great way to show wealth without actually spending a bunch of money.

Faux detailing is a clever way to add architectural details to a floor or ceiling without bothering with the expense of woodwork.

Murals add drama to a room and dress up a ceiling or a small space. Foyers and hallways are a fun and surprising place to have a mural. Of course, dining rooms are great for murals as well.

A three-dimensional mural will visually enlarge and expand the space in a room. In this way, a mural can be a focal point for a small dining area, and make the room feel less cramped.

Make sure the style of the mural art matches the style of your decor.

A trompe l'oeil wooden cornice board with real curtains that match the wallpaper design is the highlight of this morning room.

A classically inspired mural graces this hallway ceiling in a downtown inn. If you have to wait to check in, and you happen to glance up at this ceiling, I guess the mural might give you a hint that Savannah is a little bit different from other towns.

Powder Rooms

Girls, this chapter is all for you! I've used the discreet Southern term for the potty and called this chapter "Powder Rooms" because the fabulous rooms I'm showing you are not just any ol' bathrooms. These are real "pamper" rooms for women. Not that men don't need their pamper rooms, too, but they don't usually like the kind of pampering that we like.

In our house, Michael's favorite place to shower is the outdoor deck shower at the dock house. With our year-round temperate climate, he can indulge himself most any season by bathing there. I'm glad he enjoys this, but it is definitely not my thing! When I want to bathe, take a little extra time dressin' and puttin' on my makeup, or if I just want to relax and get away from everyone for a minute, I make like a Southern belle and retreat to my powder room.

It consists of one large room with a dressing table and porcelain tub, and a small toilet room. The tub is totally Southern in its old-fashioned appeal: no curtains, no showerhead, just a little side table to hold my oils and sponges and toiletries.

I like to use an indoor-outdoor rug in bathrooms—it works just as well in bath and shower areas indoors as it does out-

I love to use my hassock for dressing and pulling on panty hose. My own rug design, named Turner Creek, was perfect for this powder room. The chinoiserie cabinet is painted with gold details to match the mirror.

doors on a porch or deck. I put mine right in the middle of the powder room so that I can step out of the bathtub and not worry about drippin' on a slippery floor. A rug's a real easy way to make an overlooked room a little fancier.

I wanted my powder room to be just as pretty as a picture, so I added a chandelier, gilt mirrors, silver and crystal trays and jars, and a big hassock right in the middle where I can sit and pull on my panty hose. Now, that's what I call pampering!

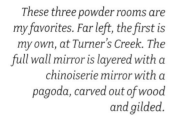

These three powder rooms are my favorites. Far left, the first is my own, at Turner's Creek. The full wall mirror is layered with a chinoiserie mirror with a pagoda, carved out of wood and gilded.

The powder room at left is Jeannie Sims's small bath that she has cleverly made to look larger with curving walls and lots of mirrors, as well as a reflective wallpaper. It just sparkles! The washbowl came from her mother's house, and is an old Sherle Wagner Oriental

design with Chinese ladies. Above, Ellen Bolch's powder room features a French cabinet that's been made into a double sink. A Venetian mirror is mounted directly onto the wall mirror, layering functionality with beauty.

Brandon's Style Secrets

Powder rooms are all about glitz, glamour, and sparkle. Make it look luxurious!

A great way to dress up a drab powder room is to add a framed antique mirror on top of a plain vanity mirror. You still have the benefit of a large mirror in the bathroom, but the antique mirror adds a touch of glamour.

Use an old sideboard for a cabinet to hold your sink, or mount a bowl on it for a farmhouse look.

Cover those ugly pipes underneath an exposed sink by skirting the sink basin to soften the look of the room.

If you don't have windows to add natural light to your powder room, mirror an entire wall to create depth and add reflected light. It will brighten the whole room.

Of course, girls, I don't mean to say that you have to have a big bathroom to be able to pamper yourself. Jeannie Sims has tucked a tiny jewel of a powder room into her little town house. The beauty is all in the details with a small bathroom. Jeannie inherited some fabulous Chinese sinks when her mother passed, so she chose an Asian-designed wallpaper that sparkles with a foil detail, and it is reflected endlessly in her big mirrors. The powder room seems much larger than it really is, and there is a lot to look at while you're in there.

I can't forget to tell you about the powder room in my little one-room dock house. The whole place is a testament to the notion that simple is sometimes best, and this bathroom is a great example of Southern simplicity. Like the sink in the kitchen, the faucet and bowl are old-fashioned farmhouse style, with lots of little details to remind me of growing up in the South. The skirted cabinet upon which the sink sits is my bow to girliness, and Michael puts up with it because he loves this bathroom as much as I do.

Y'all know I always think simple is best. This little powder room in the dock cabin is a study in vintage cottage style. The old-fashioned apothecary jars and the washbowl sink and faucet are perfect for me and Michael.

Well Behaved Women Don't Make History!

Winter

Holidays are times when my house

is full of family and friends, so I really want it to look its best. I love to decorate for Christmas, and I have traditions that I stick with each year. I have to have my keepsake ornaments on my tree, and my little handmade ornaments that have lived with us since the kids were young. It wouldn't be Christmas without all that special stuff, filled with memories!

Savannah goes all out decorating for Christmas, but mostly on the inside of the homes. You don't see much in the way of yard decorations, or lots of outside lights. Instead, wreaths of magnolia leaves, fresh greenery, and seasonal fruits are popular because they are timeless and so beautiful.

When I lived in my little downtown house in the historic district, the artist Bob Christian helped me to choose the colors to paint the walls and the double front doors. He chose a color for my door that I call "school bus yellow." You can guess how bright that door was! You could not miss my house.

When it came time to decorate for Christmas, I couldn't figure out what to put on that door that would do it justice. I finally came up with a beautiful and fragrant solution. I had two wreaths made out of live greenery and blue cedar, and decorated with fresh lemons. Against those yellow doors, my wreaths looked fabulous. The tourists would stop and take pictures of those lemon wreaths!

Once inside a Savannah home, you never know what pretty holiday decorations you'll find. When I used to cater parties here, I'd love seein' all the different sorts of things that my clients and friends in the historic district would dream up to dress up their homes. I could house hop from party to party and never find two alike! I was like a kid in a candy store seein' all those beautifully laid out tables, and the creative ways Savannahians can gussy up a room! You'll see a few examples of some fun ideas in this chapter, and maybe start some new traditions for your own house.

My Granddaddy Paul taught us that the Christmas tree had to be put up the week before Christmas and had to come down before New Year's Day, else we'd have bad luck in the new year. I'm not as good about that tradition now as I was when the boys were little. I have too many trees to take down, and too little time now. But don't worry, Granddaddy, my luck's still pretty good!

Natural greenery with fruits, ribbons, and flowers are the standard holiday decorations for historic downtown Savannah. The oversize wreath opposite is an eye-catching solution.

Live-in Kitchens

If there's one thing I know other than cookin' the best Southern food you ever put in your mouth, it's kitchens. Whenever I visit other people's kitchens, I always see something I like that I can take home to make my kitchen better. I've spent more than half my life in the kitchen, with no regrets and lots of good times. Years ago, I suffered from agoraphobia and was afraid to leave my house for a long, long time. My days and many of my nights were spent in the kitchen because that's where I could cook good things to make my family happy, and I didn't have to leave the house to do it.

Thankfully, I've overcome the fear that kept me from leaving the house, but you know what? I still live in my kitchen—and I'll bet lots of you spend so much time in yours that you feel like you do, too. I've always got a smile on my face when I'm in it—it's where the family gravitates to when they're here, and it's the center of my home and professional universe.

Because I think it's so important that everyone feel comfortable in my kitchen, it's one of the biggest rooms of the house. You don't really need a big kitchen for it to

No matter what the season, I like a bright kitchen, and flowered wallpaper, and a little vase of flowers to enjoy while I'm cleanin' up. By the way, that's one of my own fryin' pans that I'm scrubbing.

Brandon's Style Secrets

Seating is key to a comfortable live-in kitchen. Bring in a love seat or a settee for guests who need to sit when they visit. A couple of club chairs can be an inviting place to sit down when visiting in the kitchen, or a place to grab a cookbook and do a little homework for that special dinner. Couches and settees need to be durable as well as cozy and comfortable. Cover with a fabric that is wash and wear, so you won't worry about dropped sauce spoons and spilled wine.

Display your pretty tableware and bowls. Show off your pots and pans, either the ones you use daily, or the collectibles, in a prominent place. Don't be afraid to decorate this room with art, fabrics, books, and pillows, so that it is as inviting as a living room.

Bring in a dog or cat bed so your furry companions can be comfortable, too.

Keep bowls of fresh fruits, veggies, and produce on your counters so that the room looks lived in, even when you're not cooking.

Don't be afraid to put a comfortable chair in the kitchen. If you'd like a rocking chair here, then don't hesitate to add it.

be a live-in room; it just needs to be big enough to have friends and family fit in there with you. I like to have more than one table in the kitchen so that one is a casual spot to grab a quick bite, and the other will accommodate a larger crowd. The small table doubles as a cutting, mixing, all-around work tabletop, too. Mine is an old farmhouse table that I love because I don't need to worry about stains, scratches, or anything that you'd normally be concerned about with your fancy dining table. It fits my lifestyle, and it says a lot about what kind of cook I am.

You can find my Aunt Peggy, Michael,

My kitchen is a mix of old and new. A special copper hood was made for the oven to match the copper pots I've collected over the years. The antique breadbox, above, is a perfect spot to store my jams and jellies. And Bob Christian painted the roosters for me to hang over the fireplace.

This is the heart of my home—the de facto family room, dining room, breakfast room, and, oh yeah, the kitchen! The fireplace has a swinging arm for pots that I use to cook my famous baked beans.

This seating area faces the kitchen, just steps away. Bobby gave me the glass box display table next to the couch, and the majestic birdhouse in the corner was a gift from Harrah's when I partnered with them on their restaurants and the Paula Deen slot machines.

and usually one or two of the kids gathered around it drinkin' coffee any morning of the week, then at noon it will become the buffet table for our sandwich fixin's, and by afternoon it will be filled with groceries waiting to be put up, or plates set out to use for a big family supper.

I put things in my kitchen that draw people into it, like my big ol' fireplace. On a cold day with a big fire goin', I want to just stay in that kitchen forever.

Of course, no one wants to just stand around while someone is cooking, so I added a seating area that faces the stoves. If I have company that I'd like to visit with while I'm cookin', they can sit there and talk to me. Or I can put a pot on the fire, settle down on the little couch for a chat or a quiet moment to read, and I don't have to worry about runnin' back to the kitchen to check on the pot every few minutes.

I'll tell you a funny story about filmin' my cooking show in my kitchen. I was tired of showing my butt to the audience when I had to bend over to put a dish in the oven, so I bought a convection oven that is up high at eye level. I was real excited I didn't have to bend over no more, but I didn't realize until I turned it on that the motor sounds like an airplane takin' off. You can't hear me talkin' over the noise of it! So no more convection oven, and, my apologies, you still have to occasionally see my butt.

My Walk-in Pantry

My Grandmother Paul used to have a little pantry at her Magnolia Lodge and I loved to snoop around in there. She stored good things away there that she'd pull out for dinners and special occasions, as well as the everyday stuff we used when we visited the lodge.

Back in Albany when I was little, pantries seemed like somethin' only rich people had. I always wanted one as part of my kitchen, and when I designed my house on Turner's Creek, I decided I was finally gonna get my pantry. Most people think pantries are a little old-fashioned, but they never really disappeared from good Southern homes. I haven't been in a plantation house that didn't have its original pantry. My Aunt Peggy has a beautiful one that she even decorates with pretty lamps and things.

You know, a pantry can be used for more than just storing all your pots and pans and the dust mop. I keep all my pretty dishes, my sauces and spices, and baskets of fresh fruit and root vegetables handy there. It unclutters the kitchen to have a place for these things, and gives me much more tabletop space for chopping and mixing. I have a little sink for cutting fresh flowers in my pantry, too.

Shelves are a good showcase for any of my china patterns, and my "pet" pigs all seem to end up in the pantry, too. The double screened doors are reminiscent of old-fashioned pantries.

Holiday Tables

Y'all know that settin' a nice table is somethin' that I love to do. I work hard to cook wonderful food for my guests and family, and I want my Thanksgiving and Christmas tables to look good, too. I know you feel the same way.

A traditional Savannah hostess will bring out all her family silver and crystal to decorate the holiday table, and the

Holiday tables can be as simple or as elegant as you feel comfortable with in Savannah. My holiday place setting, below, consists of my china pattern, called Home for the Holidays, and some vintage-looking 1920s glasses. Brandon's table trees dress up the entire table using only a few flowers and simple greens.

The dining room chairs are the same ladderback chairs that are in the dock cabin, and go well in either setting. My farmhouse table seats the whole family and is the casually elegant look I love.

Brandon's Style Secrets

For the holidays, be sure to use all your silver, crystal, and collectibles to decorate your sideboard and table. Use a lot of candles; they are always festive.

For your flowers, use several tiny bunches instead of one big expensive arrangement. You will get the same look for less money.

If you have a garden, use freshly cut flowers for the holiday dinner table. And don't be afraid to go to the roadside and cut the wildflowers you find there. Local and fresh is always best for floral arrangements.

If you grow boxwood, clip it and make a boxwood topiary. It will look fabulous, and you've made it yourself!

Decorate with fruit for the holidays: oranges studded with cloves, or anything seasonal that you find at the grocery. It doesn't need to be ornate to be festive.

The Bolches' English hunt board acts as a sideboard for their holiday silver service. With silver and crystal this beautiful, nothing much is needed to finish dressing the table. Festive china and little bunches of red blossoms scattered around the table complete the holiday picture.

Using a blue and green motif to complement his decor, Jamie Cribbs's Christmas table is understated elegance. Lights hung on the fireplace mantel in lieu of stockings are festive and fun.

effect will be a sparkling delight. It's a formal table, but it is very Southern, too. Ellen Bolch sets one of the prettiest traditional tables I've ever seen, and her sideboard is fit for a king. You just know you're gonna remember the meal when you sit down to that sort of traditional Southern splendor.

You don't need to have a big collection of silver or crystal to set a pretty holiday table, though. There's a simple trick to sprucing up any table. Brandon has taught me that there's a thousand fun ways to decorate with flowers, without spending a lot of money or taking a bunch of time to put a pretty arrangement together.

My hairdresser, Jamie Cribbs, likes a modern decor, and his holiday table always matches his tree. The colors are different and lots of fun!

Holiday Decorating

I love a Christmas tree, and so I try to have four decorated live trees in the house during the holidays. There's the family tree, one in the living room with decorations that match our decor, one in the morning room off the kitchen, and one in Michael's and my bedroom. I like each of them for different reasons, but my favorite is the family tree because it has all the ornaments I've collected over the years: those the boys made for me in school when they were little, wonderful ornaments I've found at yard sales; even a cookie that Bobby made for me in playschool when he was four!

The thing about decorating for the holidays is that it's more fun if there's a family tradition involved. I always hang the dime-store glass necklaces that I found at a yard sale on the family tree. I love them because they remind me of prizes I won at the county fairs I went to when I was a little girl. In Savannah, a favorite way of decorating the exterior of homes in the historic district is to use garlands or wreaths of dried magnolia leaves. The leaves are large, and look wonderful with ribbons. It's a very popular Southern look.

At Lebanon Plantation, the Morrisons

Our family tree, opposite, is my main Christmas tree, hung with the dime-store necklaces that I love so much. Every ornament has a story: there's the photo ornament of the boys that I've saved for many years, and the captain ornament peeping through at the bottom of the photo reminds me of Michael; the clown with the big feet was purchased at a garage sale twenty-five years ago from a woman in her nineties who'd had it most of her life.

Savannahians don't decorate the exteriors of their homes so much, so we splurge on our Christmas trees. I have four that I decorate—each one in a different way.

The gold and burgundy colors of Brandon's living room are complemented by the colors of his tree. This room is festive any time of year, so Brandon chooses not to overdo the ornamentation for the holidays.

go all out with a fifteen-foot tree hung with bird ornaments and strung with shotgun-shell lights. It's a hunter's tree, and it stands in the great room of their lodge, framed against a wall of mounted deer heads.

Of course, all is not traditional in Savannah, and more and more often I spy glimpses of modern trees, dressed

The Lebanon Plantation's decorations are hunt-related, of course. Lifelike quail ornaments and shotgun-shell strings of lights add to the traditional grand tree. Even the deer seem to approve!

with new color combinations and frilled with feathers and other new ideas for ornaments. This is a creative town, and it isn't surprising to see all sorts of wonderful new decorative ideas as you walk the downtown streets and lanes. Square and oversize wreaths hung on doors, garlands of lights and ribbons wrapped around banisters, and palm trees hung with lights to brighten the winter night are just a few wonderful sights I see when I stroll around Savannah.

Much of Savannah's holiday style is similar to how the people of Williamsburg, Virginia, decorate, using fresh fruits on their wreaths and doors. My favorite thing to make is an apple tree, which is a wooden cone with nails protruding. I stick apples onto the nails, and top the tree with a pineapple. The smell is heavenly!

Jamie Cribbs's blue and green decor for Christmas incorporates everything in his house—from the tree with a peacock feather crown to his wrapping paper, to the garlands of lights and ornaments for the stairway banister. Ever the iconoclast, Jamie hangs a square wreath on the front door, and beribbons his foyer lamp, too. Is that mistletoe I see up there?

This invitingly modern Christmas decoration is festive, bright, and fun—and isn't that what holidays are all about?

Flea Market Treasures

Life is like a flea market: you can always find the greatest treasure where you least expect it. I'm a great believer in finding special things at yard sales, flea markets, and auctions. It's funny, but so true, that one person's trash can become another person's treasure.

Savannahians take great pride in old things, and, often, it may be something that belonged to someone else not too long ago. It's not necessary to inherit an antique to love it and make it your own. If it were, there would be no market for antiques of any sort.

And it's also not necessary to pay a whole lot of money to find things that you love. One of my prized possessions is an old wooden workbox—I think it's a carpenter's toolbox—that I found at a flea market. I use it to hold some of my silver candlesticks and other small collectibles, and it sits smack in the middle of my living room table. I love it because it's old and that makes it so much prettier to me than anything that's new. You can tell by its age and the great shape it is in that other loving hands besides mine have touched it and cared for it over the years.

I like to see how others have used

The Parkers' elegant newel post, above, is not a flea market treasure, but the antique glass doorknobs that inspired it certainly are.

Both my carpenter's box and the stack of well-worn boxes, opposite (top), are good examples of the creative reuse of old things. I put some of my more precious keepsakes in the

carpenter's box and keep it right in the middle of my coffee table so I see them every day.

The stack of metal trunks from India is the perfect solution to having a bedside table that is creative rather than boring. These ordinary items, used in a new way, give new interest and a different look to a guest room or kid's room.

their flea market treasures to decorate; it has become kind of a game to see if I can pick out the fun treasures from the real expensive antiques. Sometimes it's not so easy!

The Parker family has a beautiful glass doorknob as the finial on a staircase post, and although I have seen tons of these fabulous old glass doorknobs at flea markets, theirs was made specifically for the staircase. In this case, the Parkers had something special made because they wanted it to look like an old doorknob.

You can always pick up little tables for a song at auctions and flea markets. They are usually in great need of paint, whether they're wooden or metal. In Savannah, we don't worry about chipped paint and nicks in the wood on our flea market finds. It just adds to the age and makes it look more authentic.

My little dock house cabin is furnished with so many old things that I've had for years, and a few new flea market

Sometimes flea market finds look best when they are not repainted or refinished. The distressed table in our dock cabin was left untouched and looks perfect alongside the reclaimed wood we used for the walls. Burlap curtains with trim made from upholstery binding and big old candy jars filled with shells look pretty but don't cost a lot of money.

Brandon's Style Secrets

When you need a piece of furniture, remember that one-of-a-kind pieces can set the tone of a room. Don't be afraid to let that centerpiece to your decor be something you've found at a garage sale or flea market. Someone else's junk can be your treasure!

Garage sales are good places to find accessories that you can't always find in stores. Look for fabulous containers, vases, china, unusual chairs, ottomans, or benches.

When you decorate, keep in mind that you don't want to walk into a room and feel that it all just came straight from a stare. You want it to look like it's been collected over the years. Having fun pieces mixed into your new furniture adds depth to a room.

Don't be afraid to buy something with dents, dings, and imperfections. Make it yours with a little loving attention, or a new coat of paint. Or leave it as is and let it show its age. Savannahians love to show off the age on their furniture rather than hide it.

The great thing about garage sales and flea markets is that you can bargain over the price. Don't pay full price—haggle!

treasures that I got just recently. But the overall effect is that it all looks like it's been there on that dock for decades. I recovered my momma's old (very old!) couch. Then I found a couple of sweet little wicker chairs at a yard sale and just loved their red color too much to re-paint. I had cushions made with a burlap feel to the fabric, and hung real burlap curtains on the windows, just like a lit-tle mountain cabin would have. The walls are hung with things Michael and I have collected over the years, things that remind us of our childhood in the South—old radios, metal advertising signs, and a very special piece that I'll tell you about.

Years ago, Michael and his mother made wall hangings from old weathered planks, bits of rope, and the crabs and seashells that are so abundant around our islands. They sold them to shops on River Street, and they were so popular, they couldn't make enough of them. I am so happy that we kept one, and we make sure that it hangs in a place of honor, right where it belongs.

The crab and seashell wall hanging, left, was made by Michael and his mother many years ago. These Low Country crafts were a popular souvenir, and Michael and his mother sold them to shops on Tybee and on River Street downtown for the tourists. There are not many still around, and I always keep my eyes open at garage sales to find another one. This one hangs on the wall in our little dock house. This twig table from the 1920s, above, was a flea market find. I put a piece of fabric—left over from my living room at Turner's Creek—over the old wooden inset of the tabletop. That little swatch of fabric inspired the colors for all the rest of the cabin's furniture and curtains.

Cozy Bedrooms

If truth be known, our bedroom is not a very private room in our house, and that's okay with me (although it hasn't always been fine with Michael!). The bedroom ranks right behind the kitchen as my favorite room of the house, and I've always felt as comfortable with family, friends, and kids coming right on in and visitin' with me there as in the kitchen. There's never a "private" sign on our bedroom door.

Don't get me wrong, I like to get away and sneak a little nap sometimes during a hard workday, and I like my romantic times with Michael, for sure. I always

Our television screen slides up out of the footboard, and I admit we love to watch TV in bed! The bedroom is a calm mix of neutral colors and my second favorite room. The fabric crown over our headboard, far left, is called a pelmet.

Two bedrooms from Paula Danyluk's home show her love of simplicity and comfort. The bed at left looks like it came out of a grand French palace, but Paula made it from an antique mirror frame—she threw out the glass and tufted it to make a unique headboard. Paula keeps it simple with comfortable linens and doesn't overdo the look with too many pillows and fabrics.

The little guest room, above, is white-on-white, with just a touch of turquoise in the vintage lamp. Simple and inviting!

wanted a bedroom that would make me feel like a queen when I was in bed, and that's what I love about this room. You see, I've worked so hard all my life that I just love feelin' pampered sometimes. When I'm sittin up in that big ol' bed, I got my TV that comes up out of the footboard if I want to watch a movie or just see my latest shenanigans on air, and if any company comes along, well, they can just pile on in and watch it with us.

Once, Susan Sarandon's momma, who I'd met at the premier for *Elizabethtown*,

A guest room with a crib for the Bolches' grandchildren to use, opposite, is a sophisticated Southern mix of antiques, books, and toys. There's something for both parents and kids here.

The Bolches' master bedroom has double doors that lead to a balcony overlooking the Vernon River. The monogrammed pillowcases are simply elegant, and behind the bed is a painted antique silk screen, mounted on the wall.

The English canopy bed in this bedroom at Lebanon Plantation is the room's focal point. The combination of thick bedposts and dark woods, framed with forest green wallpaper, should make a hunter feel like he's not far from the outdoors.

Brandon's Style Secrets

Bedrooms always seem to be the last place that people decorate, when they really should be the first. After all, we spend more time in our bedrooms than in any other room.

The bedroom is a private room, so don't decorate it to be seen. Decorate it for yourself. If you love the color orange, paint the walls orange. If you want your bedroom to look like something out of a fairy tale, make it a fairy-tale room just for you. Bedrooms should reflect your wants and needs.

Don't be afraid to go all out to make this room plush and lush. Pamper yourself with lots of pillows, a beautiful bed, and fabulous linens. Even if you can't afford a fancy headboard, buy nice linens. They are an investment in a great night's sleep. A friend of mine who works at a fine linen store in Savannah says that it is usually the men rather than the women who will invest in the best linens. Businessmen who travel learn to love the feel of good sheets and pillowcases and don't hesitate to buy them for their home.

If you like lots of light in your room, forgo heavy draperies and just use shutters on your windows. The light is easy to control with shutters, they ensure privacy, and they are so very Savannah!

showed up with some of her other daughters. There were already all kinds of people at the house for a photo shoot, and we couldn't visit properly. So we just piled up in my bed and had a real girl get-together. It was fun!

Michael never knows who's gonna wake him up when they're filming at the house. I'll tell a funny story on him.

Early one mornin' when the film crew was here, Brandon played a trick on Michael. He got into my closet and put on my slip and one of my wigs (yes, I sometimes resort to wearing one!), and climbed into bed beside Michael. Brandon had me crouching by the bed, out of sight. He cuddled up to Michael, and I said sweetly, "Wake up, honey." Mind you, the film crew had gotten wind of this and was filmin' the whole thing, tryin' so hard not to laugh. Well, Michael raised an eyelid, took one look at Brandon in my wig and slip, and said, "Someone's fixin' to get their ass kicked!"

That's how private my bedroom is—not.

I have a little guest room upstairs at my house on Turner's Creek, which was originally designed to be an office, but it was the perfect spot for a little twin bed I had. My niece, Corrie, moved in with us for a while, and this room became hers. She loved the little bed because it looks like a room fit for a princess.

Savannahians have a centuries-old love for using canopies and drapery over

Rice beds like the one below are typical of old Savannah bedrooms from the 1800s. The bedposts feature carvings of rice stalks, and the canopy is typically decorative with handmade lace.

Canopies have never gone out of style in Savannah, and, on a whim, I decorated a little guest room for my niece by adding a crown with a fabric canopy to a single French daybed, opposite. Corrie loved it!

Our bed in the little cabin is a room divider, separating the living area from the dressing area in the one-room retreat. I love the reproduction ship lights above the bed, and the built-in cabinets beneath it.

Jeannie Sims works wonders with her bedroom's space limitations by mirroring the closet doors to give the illusion of greater depth. A fireplace in the bedroom is typical of the Federal-style home designs, and what a luxurious way to keep your feet warm! I also love the circular cubbyholes above the closets that hold two oxblood ginger jars. The delicate canopy of her parents' Oriental-style bamboo bed frames the small space.

their beds. Rice beds of the nineteenth century were canopied with handmade lace. I used a little crown to secure a pretty drape of fabric to cover the little daybed in this guest room. It's a modern twist on bed canopies, but it has the same grand effect.

Bedrooms need not be big rooms, of course. Jeannie Sims has room in her little bedroom for a rice bed, a fireplace, a seating area, and mirrored closet doors that double the feeling of space.

Southern Hospitality

I've been busy these last few months with a lot of new projects, and one of my favorites is building my new house. Michael is overseeing all the work, and the first thing that was finished on the new house was Michael's garage, so he could store all his stuff; he calls it the "Garage Mahal." It was really his project start to finish, but it's real nice and if I ever do a book about how to store tools and boats, it will be at the top of my list to show you!

As I write this book, our two wonderful guesthouses have just been finished—I had to have 'em, y'all! You see, I love to have family and friends around, and it seems like the house is always full, just the way I like it. So when I got to thinkin' about what I wanted to build when I planned this new house, I thought it would be great to have two little, tiny guesthouses that would be nice, private places for people to stay.

Y'all know that lots of my shows are filmed at my house, and it is just not always fun for guests to have twenty or thirty people trompin' around early in the morning, hanging lights and yellin' orders at everyone to get ready for filming.

These little houses, set just a little bit away from the main house we're building,

This guesthouse is partially furnished with furniture from my home collection, most of which is inspired by Savannah styles. This photo shows me leaning on an Asian-inspired chest, but I've taken it a step further by painting the trim with gold details to match the chinoiserie mirror. I like to add a little personal touch to everything in my home, so I'm quick with a little trim paint if I think something needs it.

My 650-square-foot guesthouse is a perfect place to show off my favorite pieces of furniture.

will solve that problem and let my guests sleep a little longer and even enjoy a quiet cup of coffee at the start of their day.

Each guesthouse is small, only 650 square feet, but you would never guess it from seein' them! The big front porches—complete with rocking chairs, of course—add another 170 square feet. I know that still sounds little, but the point of a guesthouse, I think, is that you want your friends to be comfortable—you just don't want them to be so comfortable that they move on in!

My friend and designer Carolyn Hultman furnished each of the rooms using lots of my own furniture designs. The pieces mix well with all my old things—chairs I've had in other homes, and things I love and want to recycle in a new place. And, I have to confess, there's lot of my yard sale finds in them, too, along with artwork from local and Low Country artists.

Carolyn and I decided that each guesthouse would be unique, and they are really as different as night and day! One has a casual, coastal feel with pale blues and whites, lots of shells and light. The other is more formal, with dark woods, an Asian theme, and boy, it is very el-E-gant! I think of them as my city house and my country cottage. I don't know which I like better, but I betcha I'll have fun figuring out which place each guest should go. Do you know what I mean? I'll just know that my Aunt Peggy is gonna love the Oriental one because her whole house is decorated in

I love to paint and glaze old cabinets like this one, above, to give it a distressed look.

The bedroom opposite is in my other guesthouse, and features another look that I love—casual, beachy, and comfortable. All the furniture in this little house has an antique feel with a little distressing.

that style. I think she will feel right at home when she stays with me now.

On the other hand, I'll bet my agent, Barry Weiner, would feel right at home in the country cottage. I like people to be happy when they're stayin' with me, but to be truthful, we're kinda afraid that Barry will like the cottage so much that he'll become a permanent guest!

I must praise the whole team that helped me build these guesthouses, and my architect, John Deering, who has worked with me on other projects. Isn't it wonderful to work with people you know and trust? How about this: Michael's brother Nick Groover and his partner, Troy Thomas, are our builders. I have been blessed with such a good group of people to work with.

Savannah's style is a grand mix of old and new, with the emphasis on family and comfort. The best advice I can give you about how to decorate a home is to create one that feels family-focused, comfortable, and fun. Find the sort of furniture that you feel comfortable living with— things that don't look new and shiny but have the loving patina of age. Look for one-of-a-kind pieces that you can mix and match with a lot of different styles.

When I put our home together, I incorporated the colors and styles that I love from Savannah and the Low Country so that I can share a little bit of Savannah style with you, too.

Best wishes, y'all, from me and my family to yours!

In the casual Low Country guesthouse, shutters inset into an arch serve as a room divider and allow for better air circulation. The painting of a fisherman is by local artist Jill Ferree. This room is a great place to show off my shells, too.

FURNITURE

Paula Deen Home
www.pauladeenhome.com
The Web site features Paula Deen's collections of home and office furniture inspired by life in the South and her philosophy of casual, comfortable living—style that brings comfort home! A list of participating dealers and stores is available.

The Paris Market & Brocante, 912-232-1500,
www.theparismarket.com
Located in the heart of Savannah's historic district, this irresistible shop features home furniture and decorative collections. The quirky pastiche of styles includes the Italian hip of Milan, Rome, and Florence; the wacky fun of the English countryside, London wharfs, and famous Portobello Road; and the flea market high style of Hungary, Holland, and Belgium.

Arcanum, 912-236-6000,
www.arcanumsavannah.com
This small, tasteful design store showcases a mix of antiques, fine art, and new home furnishings, lighting, gift items, and accessories with a "classically modern" sensibility.

Clipper Trading Company, 912-238-3600,
www.clippertrading.com
A 12,000-square-foot showroom features Asian imports from China, Thailand, Myanmar, and Tibet, including furniture, wood carvings, religious objects, antique decorative objects, Thai root wood furniture, and silver jewelry from the hill tribes of Thailand.

DC2 Design, 800-955-2871,
www.DC2design.com
Featuring furniture, lighting, and accessories, this fun store on Savannah's main street also sells a large selection of jewelry and handbags from Los Angeles, New York, Paris, and London.

24e, 877-2SHOP24, *www.24estyle.com*
On Broughton Street, in the heart of Savannah's downtown historic district, 24e is packed with sleek, stylish furniture and accent pieces for the bedroom, living room, and dining room.

Jeres Antiques, 912-236-2815,
www.jeresantiques.com
The 33,000-square-foot showroom is stocked with one of the largest and finest collections of rare English and Continental furniture from the eighteenth, nineteenth, and twentieth centuries, complemented by a wide range of decorative items.

Crate & Barrel, 800-967-6696,
www.crateandbarrel.com
Their well-known online store, catalog business, and chain of stores offer furniture and household goods for your home and garden.

West Elm, 888-922-4119,
www.westelm.com
West Elm furniture and accessories appeal to style-savvy customers who are looking for modern, affordable design for a casual setting. You can shop online and through their catalog, and in any of their stores throughout twenty states and in Canada and Puerto Rico.

Z Gallerie, 800-908-6748,
www.zgallerie.com
Headquartered in Los Angeles, this retailer has fifty-seven stores and a thriving online business that offer a variety of high-quality, reasonably priced merchandise for the home, including furniture, artwork, lighting, tabletop items, textiles, and decorative accessories from around the world.

GARDEN AND OUTDOOR FURNITURE

Fountains 'n' Such, 912-232-1918,
www.fountainsnsuch.com
A comprehensive resource for unique indoor and outdoor furniture and accents, displaying hundreds of different fountains, statuary, benches, planters, arbors, and unique items.

Peridot Antiques, 912-596-1117,
www.peridotsavannah.com
Housed in a refurbished old gas station, this eclectic store offers tables, mirrors, seating, art, boxes, porcelain, and garden and architectural objects and antiques.

BEDDING

Pottery Barn, 888-779-5176,
www.potterybarn.com
This large retailer started with one store in lower Manhattan in 1949 and is now a nationwide chain. Home decor, outdoor furniture, and modern furniture are also available through catalog sales and online.

LIGHTING

Circa Lighting, 877-762-2323,
www.circalighting.com
Founded in Savannah in 1998, Circa Lighting offers quality lighting, lamps, and accessories that are beautiful as well as timeless in their appeal.

Frontgate, 888-263-9850,
www.frontgate.com
Started in 1991, Frontgate is one of the leaders of catalog and online shopping for home and entertainment products.

Bevolo, 504-522-9485, *www.Bevolo.com*
Located in the heart of New Orleans's French Quarter, Bevolo Gas and Electric Lights has manufactured traditional and antique lighting since 1945. Bevolo's highly skilled coppersmiths custom build each fixture by hand from raw materials, to exact specifications, creating a product aesthetically compatible with many architectural designs.

Currey & Company, 877-768-6428,
www.curreycodealers.com
This circa 1980s company creates original designs for chandeliers, lamps, wall sconces, accent furniture, and garden accessories that incorporate an understanding of historic design and an abundance of imagination.

RUGS

Kaleen/Paula Deen Rugs, 888-452-5336,
www.kaleen.com/pproduct.php?page=paula-products
Paula Deen and Kaleen join forces to bring you indoor and outdoor rugs of impeccable style, fashion-forward colors, and uncompromising quality.

Macy's, *www.macys.com*
This nationwide retailer boasts a chain of department stores and an online catalog featuring a wide array of home goods, furniture, and rugs.

DECORATIVE ART, FINE ART, AND FRAMING

Kathy Jarman, 912-598-0578
Creating objets d'art, sculpture, furniture, and interiors, this regional shell artist's work is available through individual commissions, retail stores, galleries, and interior designers.

Atwell's Art & Framing, 912-238-9607
A gallery and frame shop on Broughton Street in historic downtown Savannah.

Elena Madden, 912-661-1534, *www.elenamadden.com*
A fine artist, specializing in paintings of water, Madden's work is available through her Web site and gallery.

Bob Christian Decorative Art, 912-234-1960, *www.bobchristiandecorativeart.com*
This muralist's work is available through his store and commissions for individuals and interior designers. His store is a fantasyland of original artwork, hand-painted finishes, accessories, and custom-designed furniture.

Laura DiNello, *www.lauradinello.com*
A popular mosaic artist in Savannah, her fine art is sold through various galleries and her Web site.

Christopher Radko, 800-723-5609, *www.christopherradko.com*
Radko's well-known work includes a wide selection of exclusively designed Christmas tree ornaments and holiday containers available through stores and online.

Friedman's Fine Art, 877-233-5604, *www.friedmansfineart.com*
A full-service custom frame shop and gallery in the Savannah area, Friedman's Fine Art boasts a fine selection of moldings. Conservation framing, finished corner frames, custom mirrors, shadow boxes, French matting, and all varieties of specialty framing treatments are also available.

FABRIC AND WALLPAPER

Sunbrella, 336-221-2211, *www.sunbrella.com*
Sunbrella fabrics are designed to withstand the elements, and are the ultimate in beauty, durability, and "cleanability" for all of your indoor or outdoor decorating needs.

Boussac Fadini, 678-904-2009, *www.boussacfadini.com*
Fadini Borghi's entire history is dominated by one ambition: to represent the charm and splendor of Italian-made fabrics since the fourteenth century, by specializing in damasks, lampas, silks, brocades, and Genoan velvet.

Thibaut, 800-223-0704, *www.thibautdesign.com*
Established in 1886, Thibaut is the nation's oldest continuously operating wallpaper firm. Thibaut offers unsurpassed quality and design in styles ranging from historic reproductions, toile, and chinoiserie to tropical and novelty patterns. Each wallpaper and fabric design collection contains a distinct group of designs by theme, including traditional, nautical, stripes, or toile.

STOVES AND RANGES

Viking, *www.vikingrange.com*
Viking offers a large variety of residential and commercial cooking equipment, countertops, kitchen accessories, and design resources. For information on where to buy Viking products, visit the Web site to find a dealer, or shop online.

INTERIOR DESIGN

Jane Coslick Designs & Restorations, 912-354-8602, *www.janecoslick.com*
Working out of Tybee Island, near Savannah, this popular beach cottage designer is available as a project consultant or to completely restore, design, and decorate your personal home or investment vacation house from start to finish.

Carolyn Hultman Interior Design, 912-236-0111
This busy Savannah designer specializes in commercial and residential interior design.

CHINA, CRYSTAL, AND SILVER

C. H. Brown Antiques & Silver
912-236-0732
Drop in and owner Charlie Brown will give you a personal history of any of his eighteenth- and nineteenth-century American and English silver serving pieces and decorative objects. His shop is a gem—don't miss it!

Vietri, 919-245-4180, *www.vietri.com*
The business started with one central idea: to promote the essence of the Italian lifestyle by offering a wide array of award-winning handcrafted pottery products for the home and garden.

7th Heaven Antique Mall, 912-355-0835
A popular place in Savannah to browse for antiques and collectibles.

DECORATIVE OBJECTS

One Fish, Two Fish, 912-447-4600, *www.onefishstore.com*
Proffering everything from contemporary slipcovered sofas and Swedish-style painted dressers to Côté Bastide soaps, this corner store is a delight. There's also estate sale furniture, lamps, and jewelry.

Two Women & a Warehouse
912-239-9665
The place to shop for unique and gently used furniture, as well as Swamp Creek Outdoor wooden furniture (Adirondack chairs, swings, tables, and rockers), all handcrafted in Adiran, Georgia. Lots of fun and funky home decor and lamps, too.

Seaside Sisters, 912-786-9216, *www.seasidesisterstybee.com*
You can't go to Tybee without a stop at this store, featuring beach cottage accessories, vintage and antique decor, eclectic hand-painted furniture, original beach art, jewelry, gifts, books, and cards.

HomeGoods, *www.homegoods.com*
HomeGoods offers unique home decor, kitchen essentials, rugs, lighting, bedding, luxurious bath towels, and affordable home furnishings. Shop online and at one of their many store locations.